LETTERS FROM PARIS

PIERRE TEILHARD DE CHARDIN

LETTERS
FROM PARIS

1912-1914

INTRODUCTION BY HENRI DE LUBAC, S.J.

ANNOTATION BY
AUGUSTE DEMOMENT AND HENRI DE LUBAC, S.J.
TRANSLATED BY MICHAEL MAZZARESE

HERDER AND HERDER

1967
HERDER AND HERDER NEW YORK
232 Madison Avenue, New York 10016

Original edition: *Lettres d'Hastings et de Paris,*
second half; Paris, Aubier, 1965.

LETTERS FROM PARIS

INTRODUCTION

BY HENRI DE LUBAC, S.J.

THE welcome given Pierre Teilhard de Chardin's *Letters from Egypt* has prompted us to publish the letters which he wrote to his parents with a remarkable regularity from the time he returned from Cairo in the summer of 1908 until he entered the army in December of 1914. At first, we simply thought of including a few extracts rather than every letter. But the public demands to know everything about a great man, and there is a very good cause for such curiosity. Thus, with the consent of the family of Father Teilhard, we have decided to publish the entire text, even though a few of the letters do not tell us very much about their author.

For four consecutive years, from 1908 to 1912, Pierre Teilhard was in Sussex, England, at the scholasticate of Ore Place, near the town of Hastings. Following the normal course of studies to become a Jesuit, he completely devoted himself to theology and was ordained to the priesthood. In 1912 he was sent to Paris to study natural science (he received his licentiate and then his doctorate only after the war). There, he often visited the British Museum, an ideal place to begin his scholarly career. Since he had not yet been drafted into the army in the autumn of 1914,

7

he spent two months in seclusion at Canterbury and then joined the barracks of Gribeauval in Clermont-Ferrand. It was also in December at Clermont that the first letters to Marguerite Teillard were begun. Thus the reader will be able to follow, almost day by day, the life, travels, work, and, to some extent, the thought of Pierre Teilhard from August, 1905, to September, 1919.

During his years of theological study young Pierre kept in close contact with the scientific milieu of Cairo. He took advantage of his vacations to explore the local flora and fauna both living and fossilized. He sent his findings to the British Museum, the Geological Society of London, and Cambridge University, as well as to the lesser known societies of Hastings and Jersey. In 1909 he spent a month's vacation prospecting the countryside of Jersey, and in 1910 he worked in a laboratory in Holland. Afterwards, he took part in a geological and pre-historical expedition in Normandy, Spain, and the Alps. After 1911 he also exercised his priestly duties: giving retreats, Lenten preaching in Pas-de-Calais, Gap, and Lyons, and distributing alms in a Parisian suburb. These activities tested "the power of the priesthood to counsel, console, and draw closer to God."

Unassuming in his ministry, he became more involved in his scientific studies. He knew his father and brothers were very interested in his work, and therefore his daily routine, news of the family, birthdays, his thoughts about contemporary events, details of his walks and travels occupy a great part of his letters. Picturesque descriptions abound here as they did in his *Letters from Egypt*. Those who know the English countryside of Sussex and Kent will recognize the charm of its hills, valleys, its small villages, its old castles, and large parks. Pierre Teilhard sees it all, both as painter and scholar: it may be a hillside in the spring, a ceremonial procession, a storm at sea, some farmers at a fair, some herons building their nest; forms, colors, and movements are all recorded with precision. One day, a herd of cattle blocked his way: he knew there were sixty-three.

It was during a walk about the outskirts of Hastings in May, 1909, that he met the amateur geologist Charles Dawson. The two found each other good company and became friends. Three years later, on April 26, 1912, a letter mentions the recent visit of Dawson to Ore Place: "He brought me some pre-historic remains (silex, an elephant's tooth, and one from a hippopotamus, and even some fragments of a human skull, which were very thick and well preserved) which he found in some alluvium deposits not far from here, in order to entice me to go out and do the same; but I hardly have any more time for that." Nevertheless, towards the end of May Pierre Teilhard accompanied Dawson for the first time to the area of Piltdown, near Uckfield; they were joined by Professor Woodward, the director of the paleontological division of the British Museum. While Dawson found a new fragment of a human skull, Teilhard found an elephant molar: "This first elephant tooth made me feel like a hunter after his first catch." On August 30, 1913, the three hunters found themselves at the same site on a new expedition. It was on that day that Pierre Teilhard had the "good fortune"—or bad fortune—to find "the canine tooth from the jaw of the famous Piltdown Man." Before he died in 1916, Dawson completed his findings during the winter of 1915. A controversy over the *Eoanthropus dawsoni* lasted a long time. Boule, at the Museum, was skeptical, or, more frankly, negative: for him, if the skull was human, the jaw and teeth uncovered by Dawson were too ape-like. Others, such as the German Weinert, thought that the problem was insoluble. Proof finally came in 1953. The jaw and teeth were shown to be fake. Father Teilhard congratulated Oakley for his discovery and wrote on December 8: "It brought back many fond memories of my youth. But this is so much more satisfying. Anatomically, as Boule had thought since 1913, the *Eoanthropus* was a monster. Then, too, how could you have explained such a strangely 'primitive' form having been found in northern [southern] England? . . . Nothing seemed to 'fit' together. It's better that it all fell through."

His letters from England not only included questions of geology and pre-historical data, but also matters of botany, entomology, and ornithology; theology was not mentioned nearly as much. Not once is any faculty member of Ore Place mentioned by name. There are some allusions to school exercises or preparations for an exam, but none is really sufficient to tell us much about the essential work of Pierre Teilhard. A casual mention about the "death of poor Tyrrell" or the first "delivery of a sermon, ordered by Pius X," does not give us a very clear picture of life in the scholasticate during this time of reaction against modernism. Nor can we tell what were his thoughts about doctrinal matters of his day. But we must not be deceived by the absence of such information. Theology was highly honored at Ore Place and everyone seriously devoted himself to its study . . . a seriousness that would seem superhuman today. Pierre Teilhard had some professors who were truly distinguished in their field. It will be sufficient to name a few: for fundamental theology, Frédéric Bouvier (a victim of the war of 1914), chosen to succeed Père Léonce de Grandmaison, who had just been called to Paris, to direct the main house and the review *Etudes*; in sacred scripture, Albert Condamin, whose severe exegesis left his students speechless; in dogma, Xavier Le Bachelet, as learned as he was a good dialectician. Among Pierre Teilhard's fellow students who were also his friends were Pierre Rousselot, who had just defended his now famous thesis on *The Intellectualism of St. Thomas* at the Sorbonne, and who would return to Paris in 1912, where he died in 1915; Auguste Valensin, whom he knew since their days in the novitiate at Aix-en-Provence and who had been his classmate in philosophy and who had probably introduced him to the works of Blondel and Newman; Joseph Huby, who had prepared a promising new anthology, *Christus, A History of Religions;* Guillaume de Jerphanion, already a specialist in iconography and the history of Byzantine art; Pierre Charles, who would often put his authoritative knowledge of dogma to the service of Teilhard's ideas, for their propagation and for their defense; Félix Pelletier, his devoted companion on scientific expeditions; Auguste Décisier, both his provincial and faithful advocate; François Charmot, who will ever remain devoted to his memory; Victor Fontoynont, his dear friend, as understanding as he was independent, his intimate confidant whose exile from China will joyfully bring them together again on a hill in Fourvière.

It was in this milieu, then, that Pierre Teilhard was also making great strides in theology. For four consecutive years he was chosen to take part in one of the "solemn disputes" of the year. The first time was in order to attack his professor's theses; the other three times he had to defend them. It was here that he proved to be a capable and practical theologian. Although he was hardly interested in living in an "ivory tower," he never

11

neglected his academic disciplines. Whenever he had to criticize —for example, when speaking of certain professional theologians as being "hemmed in by their philosophical categories," or of professors who would "do well to take a sabbatical" like the one he was on, on an ocean liner in the midst of every type of unbeliever—he began by absorbing and knowing the subject well; his reactions were not as negative as many believed: there were a number of opinions which were taught or suggested to him at this time of which he was quite fond and about which he tried to learn more, notably in Christology.

"Time spent at theology," he wrote one day, "has the advantage of making ideas mature well." The reference here remains vague. We learn little about his studies and theological convictions from these letters. They do little to show us the innermost feelings of his soul at that time. One should not be surprised that there is no direct link to *Creative Evolution,* because this work of Bergson, although "avidly read," was only for effect, "to stir up for the moment, and only for a short time, the fire which already devoured his heart and soul"—and furthermore, since the book appeared in 1907, he could very well have read it before coming to Hastings. But only a few hints of such a devouring fire are disclosed here. One does not yet sense the trembling of the vital "discovery" which is told to us in *The Heart of the Matter.* Edited under that title in 1950, that is to say, about forty years after the events took place, the memories of Father Teilhard may be lacking in some details, and more anxious to explain the origin of his ideas than to tell us about himself; yet the narrator was not afraid to arrange them in a rather schematical fashion. However, his first writings at the time of the war are quite accurate: as early as before 1914, the "discovery of evolution," in its widest sense, was for him established fact. When Teilhard tells us then that this "profoundly drifting, ontological, universal awareness" around him is growing in his mind "less as an abstract notion than as a presence" and finally "pours over his entire being," we must believe him. We notice only that he himself doubly corrects his claim, or, if you wish, adds two features that tone it down somewhat. He notes at first that it is only "little by little" that he made this discovery, and in the beginning, he says afterwards, "I was far from understanding it and clearly evaluating the importance of the change that was taking place in me."

"All that I remember from then on (and more about this magic word 'evolution' which kept coming back to my mind as a refrain, a delicacy, a promise, a call . . .), —all I remember, I say, is the extraordinary hardness and power that overtook me at this time in the English countryside especially when I was lying in the sun, when the forests of Sussex were filled with the fossilized life for which I was searching on the cliffs of Wealden clay. Truly, at times it seemed as if a certain type of universal being took shape before my eyes sprung from nature . . ."

The impression described here is written with so much force that it can only be an authentic recollection. From the above details we can also expect to see an advance in his thought over the next two years. This was especially beneficial to his work at the Museum on the problem of evolution. Moreover, this type of progress will continue throughout his life as he is gradually taken up with the idea of "cosmogenesis." He will later allude to the naïveté of his youth: "It was no longer, as before, towards something 'ultra-material,' but towards something 'ultra-alive,' that I was groping to seize and affix as the Ineffable Environment. My idea of Fullness was completely changed. And it is this new standpoint that I have held and advanced from ever since."

We also learn a little about the spiritual life of this young religious from his letters. The approaching of priesthood, Marguerite-Marie's illness, the death of Françoise in China, various family incidents, all bring it to the fore. As in his previous letters, Pierre, now almost thirty years old, was still affectionate and understanding with his parents; he spoke to them about religion without frills or affectation; some of his advice which would seem pretentious from someone else, coming from Pierre Teilhard expresses a sincere and deep piety that needs no explanation. No theories are proffered, nothing that resembles an outline of the organized doctrine that he will teach in *The Divine Milieu;* but in each circumstance there is a definite reminder of principles that will never cease to guide his own life. "God alone is the End of all things"; . . . "the good life is that which fulfills God's plans"; . . . "His will is the only absolutely necessary and most valued thing on earth; it alone is permanent and takes precedent over all." We must "see the hand of God in every event." All separation, all proof (he will say later: all passivity), must lead to "Him who must grow in us, filling up the vacuum that is left; He alone is capable of achieving this." That is what he will say over and over to his father and mother, as he will say again and again to himself, as he will repeat to everyone.

When, after the experience of the war years, Pierre Teilhard will work out his scientific and apologetic work "in forty years of continued reflection," he will not have to deny, nor even modify, these fundamental truths. All the rest, which he only caught a glimpse of before 1914, will serve, so to speak, as prolegomena. He will continue to establish a firmer foundation for them and bring them into greater clarity. It is in this fidelity to the "Necessarily and Sufficiently Unique" that he will live and die.

1

† *Collège du Sacré-Coeur, Antoing*[1] [*Belgium*]
Friday, August 23, 1912

Dear Father and Mother,

I write this in a very depressing time, . . . which I hope does not rub off on you. Since this morning it has done nothing but rain. From my window, adjoining the fortress, the Scheldt, fringed with cement mixers and cluttered with barges, looks very sad under a gray sky. Since there are no quarries I can happily delve through the many books that good Father Cugnien so generously loaned me!

My note to Joseph gave you most of the facts about my trip, which wasn't too different from any of the others; but here are a few more details anyway. In Paris I had the pleasure of arriving just in time for the opening of the subway, so I was able to

1. Father Teilhard received his new assignment on August 15. He will go to further his scientific studies at the Museum de Paris and from October on he will live at 13 rue du Vieux-Colombier. Before this he attended to his priestly duties at Orcines, his home parish. From there he went to Belgium to be near Father Edmond Cugnien, professor of natural history at the College of Antoing.

17

get to rue du Regard quickly and economically. There, as usually happens, I unexpectedly met a few old friends. One was Neyrand, the Assyriologist, who had a beard the last time I saw him and was bound for Beirut. Now he was cleanshaven and headed for the Biblical Institute in Rome (which would take him away from his second greatest passion—cricket). Another was de Vregille[2] (Mongréen from the time of Albéric), who will be my table companion at meals until January. There was also Father du Passage,[3] but he is permanently in Paris. I spent the morning with the first of the three; we visited St. Séverin, while walking by the Sorbonne, and on the way I was horrified to see wide avenues, lined with chestnut trees from Luxembourg, completely black and bare; what a difference from Sarcenat!

At one o'clock I left from the North Station. I didn't see anything of Lille, and by 5:30 p.m. I was in Tournai. Of course, I went to visit the cathedral; it made a particular impression on me from a distance against the skyline of Antoing. Its many dark blue steeples stood out against a clear blue sky. The opposite side of the sky wasn't at all clear and it was pouring by the time I arrived at seven o'clock.

Since you know the castle I won't have to describe it. Just let me say that I think it is wonderful. I never tire of looking at its powerful towers, old, stern, and severe. For example, the park strikes me as being terribly sad, probably because it lacks a good extended view of the countryside. I moved in on Wednesday; yesterday I visited a quarry (that of Crèvecoeur, at one end of

2. Father Pierre de Vregille (born in 1875), professor of microbiology and parasitology; scientific researcher for *Etudes*.
3. Father Henri du Passage (1874–1963) who was for a long time director of *Etudes*.

the park—this might interest Joseph) where I found plenty of trilobites, today I've shut myself in. Father Cugnien is on retreat until Sunday. Monday, I think we'll be taking a trip together, —which will be a treat for me. In one of the books he loaned me (Haug's *dernier cri* on geology) one of the first things I came upon was a clipping about Perrier!

Although it's perfect here I can't stay forever. I think I'm going to Louvain (11 rue des Récollets) next Wednesday or Thursday. I'll write you from there.

Having said this much, let me tell you what a wonderful two weeks I spent with you. It sure doesn't take long to get used to Sarcenat again! But then, that is no longer where I should be. Though I am not with you, you know you have all my love. To see you all again couldn't have made me happier. It would not have been right for me to lengthen my stay. Though short, it did us all some good and brought us together again as a family, which has indeed been blessed by a good God.

I received the note from Mother yesterday; thank you. It will be a year tomorrow that you were at Hastings. Now after a holiday, I must get back to work.

Adieu, dear Father and Mother. I kiss you and I pray for you.

Pierre

2

Louvain, Wednesday, September 4, 1912

Dear Father and Mother,

I've been here almost a week, but what a week! It was the
"Ethnological Week"[1] and it ended this morning. I was so
caught up in the activities that I didn't have time to write you.
But now to pick up where my last letter left off. My final days at
Antoing were most interesting, thanks to Father Cugnien, who
really knew the countryside of Tournai. As soon as his retreat
ended we ploughed through the region of Fontenoy together, in

1. See Pierre Teilhard de Chardin, "Pour fixer les traits d'un monde
qui s'efface. La Semaine d'ethologie religieuse de Louvain," in *Le Correspondant,* November 10, 1912, t. 249, pp. 553–560. The main pro-
ponents of this first Week were Father W. Schmidt, of the Society of the
Divine Word, director of the review *Anthropos* (Vienna, Austria) and
Father Frédéric Bouvier, S.J., who, since 1908, had replaced Father Léonce
de Grandmaison at the scholasticate in Hastings. (Father Bouvier was
later killed during the First World War.) The Week had been announced
by Father Grandmaison in the *Recherches de science religieuse* (t. 3,
1912, pp. 368–370). Father Benoit Emonet also took note of it in an
article in *Etudes,* October 5, 1912, t. 133, pp. 83–100.

search of quarries rich with fossils I had never seen. Finally, we went to Mons where there are curious and famous beds of chalk rich in phosphate; Father Cugnien was as ignorant as I of the locality, but finally we found the best places, including deposits from coal mines where there were great quantities of fern, signets, calamite, etc. We returned loaded down like pack-mules, seeing that Father Cugnien, despite my objections, made up his mind not even to throw out one enormous oyster, even though he already had three in his bag; —the town of Mons itself? I only got to see the railroad station and the outskirts of town. The latter were extremely picturesque (and very sad), bristling with huge, cone-like mounds of mining waste, easily reaching 150 or 200 feet high; I had the strange impression I was in the desert near Cairo with its pyramids all tarnished and clouded.

Yet the weather was very good. Hardly any rain at all, one of two such days out of the last two weeks.

When we returned to Antoing, Father Cugnien showed me where de Villele changed a rabbit into an otter; but Joseph must know that.

I left Antoing on Thursday, the 29th, and arrived at Louvain three hours later, coming right in the middle of the "Ethnological Week," which had begun on the Tuesday. In the end, the week was a success and the consequences could be very important, if, thanks to the impetus given to it and if it's continued, our missionaries seriously decide to make a documentary for us about primitive religions. Scarcely anyone knew about them ten years ago except through the tendentious accounts of evolutionist writers.

It was a heavy schedule: five intensive lessons every day. But

21

we certainly learned more here that was valid and new than in any "Congress of Religions." Except for Bishop Le Roy[2] and M. de Grandmaison,[3] I don't think you know any of the others who spoke; but they were all authorities in their own field. There were about 100 to 110 in the audience, almost all priests (French, German, Dutch, Belgian, English), belonging to a number of orders or congregations (Dominicans, Redemptorists, Franciscans, canons, foreign missions from Paris and Scheut [Belgium], White Fathers, etc.); many were missionaries; but many were also professors, and they conscientiously enlightened each other. The "Week" is to take place again next year.

Because of the "Week" I didn't spend much time in town, where everyone was excited about the fair and the merry-go-round, which even had a few wooden automobiles and even a real airplane. I don't have to tell you about a crowd of Flemish out on a spree.

Two years ago, I told you that our house in Louvain was very old and very big. It is filled with memories. For instance, the body of Lessius[4] (who taught there, or rather in a house which

2. Albert Le Roy, missionary to black Africa and superior general of the Fathers of the Holy Spirit.

3. See Jules Lebreton, S.J., *Le Père Léonce de Grandmaison* (Paris, Beauchesne, 1932). On these accounts with Father Teilhard in the years that follow see Teilhard de Chardin, *Ecrits du temps de la guerre,* pp. 89, 202, 305, 365–366, 385.

4. Leonard Lessius, S.J. (1554–1623), taught at Douai, then at Louvain; his most famous works are *De Summo Bono* (1616) and *De perfectionibus moribusque divinis* (1620). See Sommervogel, *Bibliothèque de la Companie de Jesus* (1893), t. 4, art. "Lessius," cols. 1726–1751. It is in the Museum Lessianum, a collection named in his honor and directed by the Jesuits of Louvain, that *Le Milieu Divin* of Father Teilhard was published.

has been taken from us), the heart of St. J. Berchmans,[5] one of his manuscripts, and a letter of St. Aloysius Gonzaga[6] . . .

I also met a great number of friends there from Ore and elsewhere, and the reunion was wonderful.

Tomorrow, I'm going to Charleroi, with a Belgian priest who is a specialist in carbon deposits, to see some drillings; from there I go to Marneffe, where I stay until Monday, the 9th; then I go to Florennes (the College of St. John Berchmans), and from there I'll leave for Enghien around the 15th, my last stop before Paris. I'll write you from Florennes.

I've received all your letters. My best to everybody. All my love and prayers.

Pierre

P.S. The scholastics from Louvain have an aviary in which a California partridge spends all its time bullying some pheasants four times as big as he is.

5. St. Jean Berchmans, S.J., born in Diest (Brabant) and died in the scholasticate in Rome in 1621. See H. Delehaye, *Saint Jean Berchmans* (Paris, 1921).
6. This patron saint of the young continues to be the object of a number of historical studies. See the review *Archivum historicum Societatis Jesu, Index generalis*, pp. xxi–xxx (1952–1961) (Rome, 1963).

3

Dear Father and Mother,

It's been a long time since I've written you. And since I've been moving around quite a bit, it seems to me as if it's been a month since my last letter. I mailed it from Louvain on the closing day of the "Ethnological Week." I'll pick up from there. On Thursday the 5th, in the early morning, I left for Charleroi with Father Schmitz, a rugged Belgian who knows everyone, has traveled all over the world, and was a geological consultant in a mining venture. For once I knew how great it is to travel with a man who knows the whole world like the back of his hand. Aesthetically, the rest of the trip was a waste, except for the hills of Brabant when we passed by the beautiful ruins of the abbey of Villers. A car was waiting for us at Charleroi with two engineers and some provisions to take us quickly to the drilling site, which was located on the upper side of the south end of town in a very pretty and heavily wooded section from which this coaling town seemed quite picturesque from afar. Under such favorable conditions I found great pleasure in getting past the gates which

24

block off the mysterious work of drilling. It's usually impossible to get through. They were already 3000 feet down. That is to say, the drills (which had diamond drilling heads) took three hours to go down or bring up the sample ore, which at those depths was no more than 2½ or 3 inches in diameter. The day was spent in cracking ore samples from the preceding months (they only went down 20 feet a day; drilling like this costs 100,000 francs), and in taking note of the strata. I saw a number of fossilized plants in the samples and had enough time to learn the difference between the "roof" and the "wall" of a coal-bed. Then, stopping work for a while, we all went over to an open shed for a gigantic meal, heated up on the diesel machinery! I had never seen Father Schmitz, dressed in his work clothes, so happy, joking and kidding with his engineer friends (one was called Beulemans!) undoubtedly from Brussels.

With night coming on, I went to the college to sleep and about 10 a.m. the next day I was at the very famous Marneffe in the middle of a group of old friends. The first night I had to pay a visit to the ponds and boats. The following day I began to explore the countryside by going to the woods of Moha (let this be said for Gonzague) where I noticed there are some snakes; that evening the weather changed and was bad for practically the whole of my stay there. But I went out anyway, thanks to my clerical habit, which didn't get too dirty, and dried out between trips; but the country was in sad shape; huge fields of oats had just been left there and now were so ripe that the tops of the shoots were green. But I had a beautiful afternoon anyway; my last night I visited some narrow and deep coves near Huccorgne. There the memory of Gonzague and especially of Victor wouldn't leave me; I saw Victor's teachers; his new supervisor, Father

Gohier, is one of my best friends and he should like him. I hated to leave on the 16th and not go to Strée but I had to. From Marneffe I came to Florennes, to the college of the province of Champagne. I'm enclosing a picture postcard of it and have marked out my window with an X. Aside from some crazy fire extinguisher that somebody set up on the tower, it's a pretty enough castle and was once the property of the dukes of Beaufort; the park is very beautiful. It's large, well arranged, with long rows of hedges and some very beautiful trees; half of it was set apart for the living quarters of the novitiate and juniorate of Champagne. Florennes itself is a very small rather inaccessible town, and although it is right in the middle of one of the plateaux, the neighboring regions are very beautiful: the district of Divan and the great Ardennes. First of all, I was pleasantly surprised to meet a number of friends whom I had known in Gemert in 1910, and Father Tailliez, a friend from Jersey. His brother was in the corps of naval engineers and now directs a gunpowder factory near Brest.

From Florennes I made three extremely interesting trips: two to the Meuse and one to Maredsous. To get to the Meuse, which was my main objective, I first had to go to Givet and then take the train to Mézières. The first day I examined Vireux-Haybes, which gave me the chance to see all the inferior Devonian remains (with some interesting fossils) and its contact with the Pre-Cambrian age to Fépin (this for Gabriel); yesterday, I was further south, from Laifour (where they have some magnificent fried foods) to Deville (Pre-Cambrian slate impregnated with porphyry). Geologically, it's a unique section of the country that has to be seen to be appreciated for its "prehistoric" features; all along the valley there are shales which are incredibly jagged and crumpled. Aesthetically, the region isn't bad either. The Meuse, scarcely bigger than the Allier, at times has barely enough room to flow between two sheer cliffs, 600 to 900 feet high, covered with thickly growing bushes which extend into the great forests of the Ardennes. A railroad and a road wind along the Meuse as best they can. Where the valley widens a little, there is a little village that is quite colorful with its gray houses and pointed roofs. But unfortunately, there are quite a few factories that profit by their location on the river. I had a marvelous time on both my trips. From Givet to Florennes the countryside rolls along monotonously but is very charming because of the great forests and pastures. In Givet I greatly enjoyed seeing the artillery men again; the town is very small but is surrounded by a very pretty panorama: near Charlemont and from afar, in Belgium, you can see the castle of Argricourt.

I also mentioned that I went to Maredsous: it's a famous Bene-dictine abbey, built about forty years ago by Desclée as a German monastery for some cloistered order (Maredret); it's half way from Dinan on the side of a steep ravine, built up over the centuries by the magnificent limestone of the region. As you ap-proach it, it seems as if you are walking into the Middle Ages. I went last Sunday in order to be there for high Mass; the Gothic chapel is beautiful but a little too gaudy, and every motif so often seen in Desclée publications can be found there. The offices were truly impressive; this visit made me understand the meaning and usefulness of monastic orders. It was also to me in my work. Besides the notable historians like Dom Chapman and Dom Maurin, Maredsous has an eminent geologist, Dom Grégoire, who gathered a unique collection of large carboniferous sea-urchins, which were found in a neighboring quarry. I ate

27

in the community's refectory with about fifteen other guests; hospitality is a Benedictine specialty. In Maredsous they also give a very "chic" and English education to eighty students (no more).

Tomorrow I leave for Enghien (St. Augustine House).[1] I think that there I will receive Mother's last letter. I hope she and Guiguite won't be angry with me for not writing, nor the boys: I have too little time. But I don't forget anyone and pray for you each morning.

All my love.

Pierre

P.S. 1. In Laifour I saw a poster: "Gift of Michelin. Thanks"
. . .

    2. The Lazarists have been rebellious until now at the Ethnological Week.

    3. Guiguite could have kept the book from Lourdes longer.

    4. There's a stuffed squirrel here, which was killed in the park.

1. Theological house of studies for two of the four French provinces of the Society of Jesus. Returning to France (Chantilly) after the Second World War, it is now merged with the one in Lyons-Fourvière. See *Establissements* . . . , t. 2, art. "Enghien" (P. Delattre). *Ibid.*, art. "Florennes" (G. Huvelin and P. Delattre).

4

Maison St. Augustin
3, rue des Augustins
Enghien [Belgium]

Dear Mother,

This morning, when I was saying the Mass of Our Lady of the Seven Sorrows (a feast which is celebrated today only in the diocese of Tournai), I thought of you and all your cares and troubles. I asked Our Lady to help you offer them up to God; but I must tell you that, knowing how much Our Lady suffered, I didn't dare insist too much that Our Lord take on all your problems right away. My poor Mother, you must find at times that it is really an effort to keep on going . . . But strengthen yourself with the thought of what happy results will come of all your suffering. Through it we are united to the suffering of Our Saviour and to Our Lord Himself. Let us keep it in mind and know that in spite of all appearances, the most difficult times are those we spend living well.[1] Besides, it will all come to an end. I told you in August: those last ten years, with all their sad events, are over, as if they had been the happiest ever; but it must have done a lot of good in heaven and must have helped all the souls we love and even those we don't even know. I often entreated Our Lord to help and console both you and Father, for whom also, naturally, I say all this.

One day you will see that Guiguite's accident[2] was all in God's plan, as it was when Albéric, Françoise, Louise, and Marielle were taken away from you. It's hard; but God knows.

Well, I must go, dear sweet Mother. All my love to you and Father and the boys. I'll say Friday's Mass for all of you.

Pierre

1. A spiritual principle to which he will always adhere.
2. Guiguite, during the 29 years until her death in 1936, will give evidence of her faith and courage: "The true meaning of my illness," she wrote, "is only to vanish and return in full force . . . there are three tests which are advantageous provided you put up a good fight: temptation, doubt, and illness . . . God uses illness to make us know our true selves. Get it into your head that sickness never was meant to diminish us, but to make us morally great. We should make use of it." See also "Prière du Malade très malade," in *L'énergie spirituelle de la souffrance* by Marguerite-Marie Teilhard de Chardin (Paris, Seuil, 1951), pp. 96–97.

5

13, rue du Vieux-Colombier
September 30, and October 1, 1912

Dear Father and Mother,

This time I'm writing you from my new residence, that is, from the fifth floor of a house on the corner of rue du Vieux-Colombier and rue de Rennes. My window looks out upon the latter and lets in all the hustle and bustle of the city. What's worse is the noise and rumbling of the subway every five minutes. There's a subway station right at our door. On the whole, it's pretty exciting to be perched above such a vibrant spot; as for the noise, I will get used to it quickly if I am to keep busy with all the work I have to do. Here is what's been going on: I arrived Saturday, and went to the Museum this morning. Since M. Boule[1] was not there yet, I outlined a hypothetical plan

1. Marcellin Boule (1861–1942), professor (since 1902) at the Museum of Natural History and director of the review *l'Anthropologie*. Father Teilhard paid him a visit in July (between the 17th and the 20th; see letter # 1). He brought up this first meeting at the time of his teacher's fiftieth anniversary. See *l'Anthropologie*, 1937, t. 47, pp. 599–600 (in Cl. Cuénot, *Teilhard de Chardin*, Baltimore, 1964, p. 33). "The awesome

31

with the assistant, M. Thévenin, to allow me to see some carnivorous remains from Quercy; while awaiting confirmation of my request and some study aids, that night I began to work in the library of the paleontological laboratory, where I will be spending a good deal of time. And so my year started off with a bang. The future will tell if I do well. This morning I saw my good friend from Cairo, the mineralogist Couyat: he's becoming a real Arab and spends half the year studying in the middle of the desert. I'm very glad to see him again. Also, within these first few hours in Paris, I must also add that yesterday I accompanied Abbé de Genouillac[2] to the rue des Postes, where he is going to conduct the initial retreat of the year; at this time I also

---

Boule, a native of Auvergne, was a small husky man, authoritarian and quick tempered, . . . but had a rare intelligence, was a good geologist, an excellent paleontologist, and was exceptionally brilliant in comparative paleontology and one of the greatest authorities on Neanderthal Man. Later, Teilhard will disagree with him, all the while respecting and loving him like a father. And Boule returned this affection to him" (Cuénot, p. 34). In January, 1947, in a review of the third edition of Boule's basic work, *Les Hommes fossiles* (posthumous, ed. by Henri-V. Vallois), in *Etudes,* Father Teilhard writes: "What the author defends with righteous energy (with more insistence perhaps than would now be necessary), is that the human species appeared on earth in accordance with the laws governing every other form of life: from which derives its present and past form. What he unfortunately did not see well enough (a fault which is perhaps due to his whole generation), was that this likeness in 'embryogeny' does not stop man from producing an *exception* (an exception of emersion or eminence, and not one of anomaly), without which everything remains unintelligible, even scientifically, on the Tree of Life" (t. 252, pp. 127–128).

2. Abbé Henri de Genouillac (1881–1940), philologist and archeologist, author of a number of works about Assyriology. In 1907 he published his theological thesis: *The Christian Church at the time of St. Ignatius of Antioch.*

met the sympathetic M. Mativet, to whom I could give some news about Centraux. Perhaps you know that the building is gone, but we still have one more year there: then the school will be transported to Versailles.[3]

Now I must tell you about my last ten days in Belgium. My last letter was on Tuesday, the day before I left Florennes. On Wednesday morning I started out for Enghien without rushing. First I stopped at Maredsous, not to go back to the abbey but to visit the quarries across the way where those wonderful fossils came from. You know, the ones I had admired in Dom Fournier's collection. And as Dom Fournier had told me, I saw very little, but nevertheless more than I expected. After Maredsous I stopped at Dinan, such a picturesque little town, not only because of the town itself but also because of its position on the Meuse, sheltered by high walls of rock that look like withered prunes. From Dinan to Namur, —and most especially from Yvoir to Tailfer (pretty names, aren't they?)—, the view is very beautiful; unfortunately, the villas and even a big sanatorium begin to clutter up the landscape (at Godinne). I think that the tributaries of the Meuse in this region (for example, the Lesse, which goes through the grottoes of Han) are in valleys that are even more picturesque.

There's not much you can say about the country from Namur

3. The school of Saint-Geneviève, a preparatory school for the "Grandes Ecoles," had occupied a mansion on the rue des Postes since its beginning in 1854. At the time of the decrees of Jules Ferry in 1880, the Society of Jesus ceded the school's direction to an "anonymous Society of preparatory schools"; in 1901 the last Jesuits had to leave; in 1912 when the building was confiscated they prepared to move to Versailles and open the school there. See *Etablissements* . . . , t. 3, art. "Paris, Ecole Saint-Geneviève" (H. du Passage).

to Brussels; it's very ugly except for the forest of Soignes, the remains of a great carbonized forest. The old boundaries seem to be the towns where French is spoken.

Enghien is situated on very flat land, and aside from geology it has just about two attractions: some historical memories, especially the battle (Steinkerk), and the huge park of the Arenberg princes (more than 200 hectares). The only thing that remains of the castle, which burned down towards the middle of the nineteenth century, is a mortuary chapel, rich in works of art (there are some Rubens); the park, designed in a French style, is not kept up but it has signs of its former beauty; the Enghien Fathers, as well as several other various inhabitants, have permission to walk through it, and even the scholastics, during vacations, can go fishing in the ponds which have very big carp. Despite the fact that the land is flat you can see the terrain tapering off like I had already seen in Marneffe and in the Ardennes. (It looks like the crest of a wave unfolding which starts at Huccorgne and is still visible at Caffier, which is on the top of a hill although the town is now completely destroyed.) The repetition is very interesting. In two or three places the shale is imbedded with beautiful porphyry, already well exploited. I also visited the gigantic quarry of Quenast, where 1200 laborers work in an immense amphitheatre from which come a great number of cobblestones used in northern Europe. Although liberal, the foremen have shown themselves to be very congenial.

I add for Gonzague's information that there are quite a few rabbits in this area. A whole litter hopped up to me, stared, and scurried away.

I won't write anymore today because I want my letter to arri

quickly. I did not receive Mother's last letter which must have arrived after I left Belgium. The number here, by the way, is *thirteen*.

My love and prayers to all.

Pierre

6

Dear Father and Mother,

I've just returned from Bourget where I went to say Mass this morning in a glass factory. The owner, M. Pâris (he has a son in his third year at Marneffe), is an excellent Christian who has opened an orphanage for abandoned youngsters, ages fourteen to eighteen, who work in his factory. It is with these young ruffians, who are already quite tamed by the Sisters of Charity, that I have been working. Many of them are so lonely that it gives me great pleasure to work with them. I only wonder if my work will allow me time to visit here every two or three weeks. Without realizing it you can spend an entire day. There is nothing much to do about Bourget and there are not too many things of interest except what happened back in the 70's and Pâris's house (a former hunting lodge of Louis XV in the forest of Bondy), where I couldn't have been treated better. I discovered that Mme Pâris is from a family up north, and related to the de Béthunes; but I don't know too much about genealogies and family trees to go into many more details. M. Pâris took me on a tour of his ovens where they were in the process of making decanters of various shapes and sizes. It was dark and the melted crystal took on the fluorescent tinge of the lights.

Aside from this, all I have done for the past two weeks, model student that I am, is learn the streets from the Museum to the rue du Regard (where I have my meals); I haven't even been across the Seine! Here is my schedule: at 6 A.M. I say Mass in the Abbaye-aux-Bois, which is before the ruins of the former community; then back to my room on the fifth floor of the rue du Regard. Around 9:30 I dive into the subway towards Auster-litz; work at the Museum. At 11:30 I hurry back to Regard, eat, and then return to the laboratory where I stay until 5:00. Then I return to Vieux-Colombier, usually strolling along one of the side streets. By 7:30 I am back at rue du Regard for the third time.

You can immediately say that a large portion of my time is spent in the streets. But it is unavoidable and has the advantage of calming my nerves. When school starts in November it will be necessary to work out a time-schedule so I can fit everything in.

In the laboratory I am beginning to get on with my work, and am kept busy sorting jawbones and authors. I am now com-pletely at ease with the personnel, Boule and the others, —and have made friends with the regulars, few as they are. From what I have already said, you can see that I haven't yet visited many relatives. Now it is Victor who is not going to delay. Apropos Gonzague, I saw one of my old friends today who is an ex-purser of the Navy. I asked him about a naval career. First of all, I've learned there are actually two branches, naval recruiters, and pursers of the fleet. The first stay on land and remain in the same place a long time—the second sail about the world. In either case you can advance up the ranks quickly. They are well-paid positions with good vacations, and enlistments look good. A law degree is very important since a purser handles all juridical matters. He must know English.

The competition is not especially difficult and the protection that the Navy gives the world can play an important role. It seems to me that Gonzague would not make a mistake if he wants to tackle such a job.

I am naturally very sad to hear about poor Guiguite's trouble and keep her and all of you in my prayers so that Our Lord can help you see the fulfillment of His will; it's the only thing that counts.

All my love.

Pierre

7

Dear Father and Mother,

I know I haven't written in a long while, but fortunately you've had Victor to keep you up to date on my goings-on. I don't have to tell you how happy I am at his and Gonzague's success; you couldn't have foretold which would have taken defeat the worse. Last Sunday I finally went to see Uncle Cirice, who only lives fifteen minutes from here by subway. It was very good to return to that corner of Clermont where I spent my youth. Even the two dining-room tables were still there (with partridges hanging over it by their feet); but it was also a little sad. I found that my poor uncle had changed a great deal and looked all worn out, but perhaps things will improve. All his family was there, and very merry. Aunt Marie told me she wrote to Mother, so you know that Marcel is working for the electric company, and that Alice has been accepted. I remembered Marcel, thanks to a picture Gabriel had of him. But I didn't remember Alice or Bob at all. I especially enjoyed seeing Jeanne and Marguerite again; Marguerite invited me to visit her at home; if I had done so earlier, I could have used her chapel to say Mass.[1] That would have made a lot of Teilhards.

I'm still doing about the same as before, except I'm getting to know my carnivores better, and my circle of acquaintances is growing little by little. And finally, I've almost grasped the "physiognomy" of the jawbone. Tonight I'm going to work on the collection from the School of Mines, where I've been well treated. I've also joined the Geological Society of France, which along with its many and interesting lectures, offers the use of its beautiful library and the chance to meet many interesting people. They have their first meeting next Monday. —By then my courses will also have begun: but at this point my exact program is still up in the air. Tomorrow night I'm going back to Bourget to see my little glassmakers for All Saints' Day. That won't stop me from thinking of you that day and of all our deceased relatives. Monday, I will remember them in my Mass.

I must close. My love to you all at Sarcenat. My best to Guiguite. I'll write Gabriel in a week or two.

Pierre

1. Marguerite Teillard-Chambon, daughter of Cirice Teillard-Chambon, after having received her teacher's license in 1904, at the age of 24, accepted to direct a pension for the Religious of Sion (closed by order of the law ordering separation of Church and State) and it became the Institute Notre Dame des Champs (rue Montparnasse). Cirice Teillard died on November 16, 1916. See Teilhard de Chardin, *The Making of a Mind* (New York, 1965), pp. 13–21.

8

Paris, November 12, 1912

Dear Father and Mother,

These past two weeks have certainly gone by quickly; a whole day is spent in two sessions at the Museum and now I have classes to attend, too. As for the classes, I'm not satisfied with them at all. They're not what I need and we've had a lot of it before. One of the most interesting men to listen to is Professor Joubin[1] from the Prince of Monaco's oceanographical institute. His specialty is deep-sea life; unfortunately, he must speak to people who know very little about science, and besides, his subject is just an added attraction, not what I really need. I really learn from books and conversations. I also met Dr. Obermaier, a young Austrian priest[2] who is going to direct the anthropological

1. Louis Joubin (1861–1935) was a professor at the Museum of Natural History since 1903.

2. Father Hugo Obermaier, specialist in pre-historical archeology in Spain (and Northern Africa). See letters 21 and 22. He had just published a large volume, *Der Mensch der Vorzeit* (Berlin-München-Wien, 1912), first of a three-volume work: *Der Mensch aller Zeiten, Natur und Kultur der Völker der Erde.* He was a member of the Institute of Human Paleontology of Paris.

institute of the Prince of Monaco (not yet open) with M. Boule and another priest, M. Breuil;[3] he showed me some wonderful things (stone tools, carved and sketched-out bones) which he just found in Spain, and has shown himself to be most friendly; perhaps I will learn the most from him. As for my fossils, they're becoming more interesting the more I learn about them.

I've also seen a lot of the family in the past two weeks; first of all, I said Mass for four days at Notre Dame des Champs, which gave me the chance to see Marguerite again; she is so kind. Before I left she asked me to show her and a few other "professors" the Museum; and so I had the honor of showing five or six young ladies, including Alice, the paleontological section.

I went back to Bourget for All Saints' Day, and will be going again next Sunday. Then every two weeks. The last time, M. Pâris was alone, because his wife was in Marneffe. He took advantage of it to talk to me at great length about hunting; would you believe that he managed to arrange with two or three farmers to set up a game preserve in the fields of St. Denis, four miles from Paris. Since its opening about 200 partridges and 50 hares have been bagged—and this without the addition of new wildlife. I must add that the hunt is conducted by flushing the game, and is permitted only four or five times a season. The rest of the time M. Pâris uses his park as a warren, with nets to keep the rabbits from getting out, but also with "entrances" to let those that get out back in.

My little glassmakers have also seemed very interesting.

3. Father Henri Breuil (1877–1961), who will be a professor at the Collège de France and a member of the Institute and will be nicknamed "the pope of pre-history." Teilhard and Breuil became quick friends.

On All Souls' Day I took advantage of the "bridge" and risked the gypsum quarries of Romainville; you can get to this notorious place via a direct connection from Belleville and Les Lilas (!). I easily found the quarry and the workers were quite cordial; they are used to having geologists visit them and one of them told me, poetically, that he'd found a "sardine." As a matter of fact, there are many remains of fish, along with birds' bones and various kinds of snails. I'll be returning there from time to time.

You were probably surprised to see my advertisement in the *Correspondant;*[4] I must say that in reading the proofs there was at least one spelling error, and some mistakes in punctuation, rendering at least one phrase incomprehensible. Besides, only a few would read it all the way through, anyway. Needless to say, I follow Gonzague's ups and downs with interest. Are you quite sure that the study of law *in view* of an ulterior situation, and at the same time the study of a language, would not suffice to occupy this young man's time? Nowadays a knowledge of German only is a feeble superiority.

Thank you for sending me the letter from the British Museum; it's their acknowledgement of receipt of my fossils from Hastings. It's on beautiful parchment paper. The English certainly have finesse.

My expenses with Victor amounted to eight francs, since you want to know. That and the other seven francs came from what Mother sends me once in a while with her letters.

I forgot to tell you that the Geological Society has begun its meetings; it's very interesting, especially since you can always meet a crowd of friends; you can also learn a few things.

4. See letters 2 and 9.

Goodbye, dear Father and Mother. My love to you both, and also to Guiguite and the boys. I pray for you all.

Pierre

I saw a book that would probably interest Guiguite; it's a new life of Ozanam by Bishop Baunard.[5] The style is a bit old but it is filled with lovely things.

I'll gladly look at the small brochure M. Jacquemont sent.

5. *Frédéric Ozanam d'après sa correspondance* (Paris, Poussielgue, 1912). The hundredth anniversary of his birth was celebrated that winter (1813–1853).

9

Dear Father and Mother,

Time continues to go by too quickly and I see, too, that my correspondence has slowed down. Thank you for keeping up yours; the series has been stretched this time by four big pages from Boléo.[1] Olivier has been keeping me up to date on the minerals he finds, and having concluded that he would have to own the mine Amélia, if he wanted to find anything pretty, he ends in a postscript by telling me he owns it. I'm just as happy as you over the news; and also about Gonzague's new decision. Michelin—it seemed like a pretty shabby solution; what's more, I wonder if the rubber industry in Clermont isn't already out of his reach, or at least it will be much more difficult to move ahead, not like those who started out with the firm. I now hope Gonzague will spread his wings a little; in any case, his wings won't have to be clipped for a while. In regard to my article, thanks for your money order, Mother. It arrived safely. The

1. From his brother Olivier, an engineer in the copper mines of Boléo California in Mexico.

45

editors of the *Correspondant* were also very generous: 10 francs a page.[2] Thus supplied, I spent it at Le Chevalier's, who immediately asked me if I was a relative of his faithful customers from Sarcenat. He sends you all his warmest regards.

My work is going well; only I'm coming to the point where my collection of carnivores is getting larger than I know what to do with. But it's good practice. What I like is being up front and seeing everything first-hand; the other day, M. Boule allowed me to admire in his drawer an insect-eater, preserved in marl (it looks like those from Limagne—the Oligocene period). It's covered with hair! (Imagine a dead rat in a gutter.) I'm working amidst the strong odor given off by four Mammoth feet (the bones and flesh are in another bottle), —covered with long, tow-colored hair, —which have just come from Siberia.

In oceanography Professor Joubin is always very interesting, and Professor Haug is making progress at the Sorbonne.

Olivier de Fontanges came to see me at the Museum. It was late and that made his visit short, but it was still twilight when we left. You already know I went to Uncle Cirice's for dinner. He's doing well and is fixing up a few things around the house. Once again this really shows his self-sacrificing, and he also seems to be interested in doing it. All the cousins are fine, and when Mlle Ponson began to play some old favorites I sat off, far away. Last Sunday, for the first time in my life, I went to Boulogne Park. Although the weather wasn't too good (it was very overcast), it made me feel like finding a field and some trees where you could be alone and undisturbed.

2. Stipend for the article appearing in the November 10th issue (t. 249, pp. 553–560): "Pour fixer les traits d'un monde qui s'efface. La Semaine d'ethnologie religieuse de Louvain."

My visit to Bourget, ten days ago, was very pleasant; my little glassmakers are now well tamed. On Saturday night I stopped in on M. Pâris, and found they were celebrating the birthday of one of his sisters-in-law. I was immediately invited to dinner, which made me feel like I was back in Sarcenat. I'm going back next Saturday.

Adieu, dear Father and Mother. My love to you all at Sarcenat. I pray for you each day. I'm very happy about the success of the Orcines mission.

Pierre

Can Father imagine that I daily see the towers of St. Sulpice, at least when the moon is out, just as they look in the picture he has in his room?

If you want, I could easily buy a little book, describing Boléo (about which Olivier spoke). Just send me the name of the publisher. Father noticed it while I was in Sarcenat.

10

Paris, December 11, 1912

Dear Father and Mother,

I don't have to tell you I was greatly pained to hear that Mother was ill; Guiguite was very kind to write me about it so often. Mother will just have to make up her mind to do things in a more orderly way now, and not run around for things she doesn't really need, or that someone else can get for her. I hope she won't get too tired when you go down to Clermont, which isn't too far.

I'm very surprised to see that the trimester is already starting. On the whole, it will go rather well for me; but a year is definitely too short for some things and I can see that I'll need to ask for another. Whether they'll give it to me is another question.

For some time now, I have had too much work in the paleontology laboratory; I attended several sessions of comparative anatomy and soon plan on taking a course in casting. In comparative anatomy (a dismal little trade that comes after entomology—Gabriel should know that) I've been studying horse heads, ox heads, etc. The place is filled with bottles that give off a

48

sickly odor of alcohol, and from day to day you can see what's died in the Jardin des Plantes, sometimes in an advanced condition . . . "That's nothing," the lab assistant told me. "If only you had seen it when it was a hippopotamus!"

Otherwise, I'm still not finished with Jersey. A respected local artillery captain from there is stationed in Paris and he's working with great zeal on a new geology of the island; during the five o'clock meal I contribute my enlightenment, and at the mineralogy laboratory I look at microscopic preparations that he has cut into my specimens. It gives me the opportunity to see M. Lacroix, who is very delightful.

Since my last letter I've extended my family relations. First of all, last Sunday I finally went to see Uncle Georges, whom I found peacefully seated by the fire, munching on some bonbons. It's been at least eighteen years since I've seen him, and I still had to meet Aunt Madeleine. That didn't take long. The children arrived after some time, and in their presence Uncle Georges really showed himself as a good "Papa." Françoise told me that she only likes arithmetic, and John likes algebra; Uncle Georges takes these remarks with an air of irony. Do you know that at Latour-Maubourg Square you can eat wholewheat bread like you can get in Sarcenat and in St. Nectaire (and a few other things too)? This reminds me that on a small street near Cherche-Midi, on a shabby old house, I saw an equally shoddy sign which said "Mineral Water from Ternant, Puy-de-Dôme." That probably refers to Ternant of Lembron, don't you think?

Maybe I will go to Montreuil next Sunday; it's the start, I might say, of many a busy Sunday to follow; but it's better than having nothing to do.

Next Sunday I'm also going to Bourget; now there's a trolley between here and Villette, and there you get the subway. I'm going to try it. It will probably be more comfortable and save some time. I forgot to tell you that afer Christmas I plan on going up to spend a few days at Louvain (again!), where you'll find, "by chance," half the collection I sorted out at the Museum.

Adieu, dear Father and Mother. My love to you, Guiguite, and the boys, and I pray for you all.

Pierre

11

Dear Father,

Following our custom, I write to wish you a Merry Christmas and, at the same time, a Happy New Year. It's been a long time since I've been able to say it to you in person. This time Yéyé is the farthest away of those of us on earth. In spite of the fact that you must certainly feel his absence, you will surely remember him most clearly during the ceremonies tomorrow night and on Christmas.

One of my midnight Masses will be for the family and I will especially mention you at this time. I will ask Our Lord to help us all to be your worthy children, to help us lead, not a long or brilliant life, but one that will completely fulfill His will, that is, to do what is asked of us.

God always gives more than a thorn-bush; besides the empty seats, there is Guiguite's health, and the little worries about the boys. This is what really counts, Father. With the family we had, if everything had gone along "well," we would have run the risk of not thinking enough about heaven and not wanting to leave at all. Both good and bad come and go and we are left with the future. And, between us, I think people prefer it that way. Nevertheless, I will ask Our Lord to give you a good New Year and I hope He will.

Adieu, dear Father. My love to you and to Mother, too. You know you always have my deepest love.

Pierre

12

Dear Father and Mother,

I should apologize for using such a small piece of paper to wish you a Merry Christmas; but it's getting late and I want you to get this before Wednesday morning. So, I must send it today.

I've just come from dinner at Uncle Georges' (so you will get some recent news about me when he gets to Clermont). It is a real Teilhard place and the children speak the same way I did when I was their age. In the past two weeks I've seen a good number of our relatives; one or two Sundays ago I went to Montreuil to see Aunt Pauline and Anne-Marie. Of all things, Aunt Pauline remembered my practical jokes at Vernière best of all (some frogs in her bedroom, I believe); Anne-Marie seems to be doing well, though she has time for little else than work.

All in all, I see the Cirices the most; I met them all yesterday at the du Ranquets. Good old Uncle Cirice is up to his neck making social calls; his whole family is doing well. Marguerite did me the honor of introducing me to M. de Margerie[1]; she's

1. Emmanuel Jacquin de Margerie (1862–1953), geologist. De Margerie's family was very friendly with Marguerite Teillard.

53

also given me an invitation to Amundsen's reception.[2] Although the amphitheater in the Sorbonne is large, Marcel and I had trouble finding seats. The lectures were worth it all. He spoke with simplicity and an air of coolness, probably because he didn't know French too well, but he made a good impression. When he spoke that fateful sentence, ". . . At last we were at the South Pole," the audience broke into prolonged applause—a curious example of the facility with which we magnify the importance of some things by hearing someone speak about it: there wasn't one listener who wasn't relieved at "reaching" the South Pole . . . I was able to see that Amundsen had a great amount of energy and a wonderful method. There were many films: first of all the South Pole, that is, a field of snow, —some antarctic mountains, frightfully deserted and fierce, —finally some very interesting films: a school of whales, a seal hunt, a sailor teasing a penguin, who, finding it rather bothersome, waddled off, wheezing like a goose, etc. Guist'hau[3] also spoke very well.

Right now I'm about to leave for Louvain; I'll leave Paris Thursday morning and my address for the week will be 11 (*eleven*) rue des Récollets. I still don't know exactly how long I will stay in Belgium. Tomorrow night I'm going to Bourget to say midnight Mass for my little glassmakers. Be assured that you will not be forgotten; one of my Masses will be for the family.

I must close, dear Father and Mother. I love you both, and give my love to Guiguite and the boys. I'm glad she was able to

2. Roald Amundsen, Norwegian explorer (1872–1928).
3. Guist'hau, friend of Briand, Minister of Public Instruction in Poincaré's cabinet, installed on January 15, 1912.

make the trip to Clermont without too much discomfort; thanks
for her letter.

Pierre

13

Paris, February 5, 1913

Dear Father and Mother,

It sure has been a long time since I've sent you a real letter, and it's already Ash Wednesday! The biggest news around here came abruptly last Sunday, when I was told I would have to spend three weeks in Gap instead of fifteen days.[1] I had hoped I would get only eight days. Now I have an extra week and don't like it at all; but come what may, I won't complain. Up till now I've never had anything to complain about. Only this is going to make me leave as early as February 26 or 27 which will interfere with some of my classes. I'll arrange my trip so I can return by way of Montauban and, I hope, Clermont. After that I hope to get back to some serious study, unless Quercy finds something else for me to do. Meanwhile, I'm setting aside some time for my sermons and study at the Museum; today, I was at the School of Mines, which is unusual, —it was great to go through Luxembourg twice, and I had a marvelous time

1. A priestly duty (preaching, hearing confessions, etc.) at the end of Lent was usually assigned to the young priests; Father Teilhard was assigned to a parish in Gap.

56

amidst the swarms of children. I love this little place very much.

I'm expecting Father Alphonse to be here tomorrow. He's on his way to Rodez. We haven't seen each other since 1897.[2] I really think he will sound me out on the subject of divine grace and freedom; if that's the case, he'll find I'm singularly cold to such scholarly questions.

If you should see a copy of *Etudes* at Aunt Isabelle's, the article about Turkey signed * * * is by Guillaume de Jerphanion (who is becoming more and more Byzantine) and interesting.[3]

Last Sunday I went to Our Lady of Victory and prayed especially for you. My love to you both and especially Mother. Be sure to take care of yourself. My thanks to Guiguite for her letters.

Pierre

2. Father Alphonse, a Dominican, was a first cousin of Marguerite Teillard.

3. *Lettres de Turquie: Constantinople sous le menace des allies* (t. 134, pp. 164–187). II. *Les Puissances et la Turquie* (pp. 473–491). Father Teilhard de Chardin's article on "La Préhistorie et ses progrès" is in this same issue of *Etudes*, pp. 40–53.

14

Dear Father and Mother,

In spite of the fact that Gabriel will give you many more details, I can't let this chance go by without telling you a few things myself, —especially since it's been about three weeks since my last letter.

As you know, I was very happy to see Briel again. We made the rounds, visiting the family, and finished off by spending a very typical night at Uncle Cirice's. Cécile played the piano—a piece which Guiguite used to practice diligently during the time when I was just beginning in the humanities (it was a Canzonetta, I don't remember by whom). This morning we are going to the Museum.

Like you, we too have had some beautiful cold and dry weather, which must make the farmers happy. It's lasted a week already. Last Tuesday was a very welcome day, in the manner of feting the President; that day I went on a geological expedition with M. Boussac, professor at the Institut Catholique,[1] two of his students, and an assistant professor at the School of Mines. Our goal was Cormeilles-en-Parisis, on the right bank of the Seine, across from the St. Germain forest; at this point you can trace almost all the layers of earth around the vicinity of Paris, one by one along the slabs of stone and plaster; and when an expert is pointing this out, it is very interesting to see these ancient layers of soil; I certainly won't forget them. Even though it is winter, this part of the Seine is very pretty. It has a good view and is uncluttered by villas; it's perhaps the best view I've seen in five months. Gap should change all that, unless it gets foggy while I'm there.

I leave next Thursday night; I'll be in Lyons Friday morning, will leave there at three o'clock, will sleep in Grenoble, take the 8 a.m. train, and arrive at Gap about noon. I'll let you know what happens, even if it's just a postcard. From Gap I plan on going immediately to Quercy; early in the week after Low Sunday I will cross Auvergne. But all this seems very far off, though I know it is really just around the corner and will come more quickly now that I'm busy. I will probably preach next Sunday; then twice each day the following week (to the women); then seven times to the men, at night after Passion Sunday; finally, a few other times, namely, Good Friday and Easter.

I'll send Mother a memento of it. I'm going there feeling very calm and fairly well prepared.

1. Like the great geologist Pierre Termier, Jean Boussac was killed in the war in August 1916. See *The Making of a Mind,* pp. 91, 103, 110, 116, 123, 124.   Father Teilhard will later succeed him in his chair of geology on the Faculty of Sciences at the Institut Catholique in Paris.

I hope Mother and Guiguite continue to be in good health. My love to you all and I will remember you in my Mass on Easter.

Pierre

15

Gap, March 8, 1913

Dear Father and Mother,

The women's retreat ended this morning and was less trouble
than Mother thought. There was a record number of communions; but this was due largely to the good will of the people of Gap. They weren't waiting for me to come along to bring
it out. The talks were well attended; besides, Bishop Berthet
didn't once bother me, and on Easter I'll have to remind myself
first to say "Your Excellency" before "my brothers." I went to
visit him when I arrived and found that he hardly ever left his
residence. This has been going on for a long time and it sure
doesn't help to give his diocese some life. But this apathetic atti-
tude is counteracted by some wonderful priests, and the laymen
have what it takes to become good Christians. I'm not saying a
thing about the canons. Since the separation of Church and State
the corps of canons is slowly disappearing. On the other hand, I
have nothing but good to say about the congregation. My pastor,
M. Bernard, is very young, quite frank, and a true gentleman. He
knows Paris better than I and spent two years in Thiers, as a

61

boy, where his father was a tax collector—tobacco taxes, I believe. His mother, who lives here with him and who takes care of me as though I too were her son, doesn't stop praising the kindness and generosity of the people of Thiers, which she likes to think of as a region of moisture and flat, open country. For the past week I've come to expect the unexpected. For example, to-morrow morning I'm going to harangue the Femmes Françaises; this coming week will be a little less hectic: only one sermon a day to the men. Signs have been posted in town since yester-day, a marketing day, which give the subject of my talks and which announce that Abbé T. de C. "from the clergy in Paris" (*sic*) will deliver them.

It would be good if Mother doesn't stop praying.

Father isn't completely wrong in comparing Gap to Maringues: the two are nearly on the same order of grandeur.[1] We are the only ones that have a general, a prefect, a bishop, a court of assize, a school, and a departmental museum whose curator—a little man from the mountains who is very interested in geology and who has shown some old fashioned hospitality—is already my friend. I thought it would be cold and foggy here. It's all been blocked by the Croix-haute pass (4000 feet), half way from Grenoble; ever since, the weather has been bright and sunny. At night it's usually cold; the grass, where there is some, looks dead. During the day the sun is very wonderful. But I've hardly left the town; I'll try to get out a little more this week, but won't be going too far away. It makes me sad to think that behind the ridges of the Chansore (9000 feet and more) (I ignore the orthography) are Pelvoux, Meije, and the glaciers; they look so

1. He exaggerated. Maringues, a small marketing town in Limagne, a chief district of Thiers in Puy-de-Dôme, had more than 2000 inhabitants.

close and yet I will be leaving without having seen them; but then, I didn't come for that.

Gap, like Issoire, is a departure point for the mountain railroad; you can see the "express" train for Barcelonette leave in a cloud of dust every day (like the auto from Sauxillanges): It gives the impression of being very far away. It appears that some officials, who were sent here, even packed some matches in the luggage! But they're wrong.

I am receiving all your letters. Thank you.

My love and prayers to all. Give my best to Guiguite.

Pierre

16

Dear Father and Mother,

You've probably been waiting for me to write. I haven't had any free time for the past week.

The last time I wrote you it was Holy Thursday. Right now it's the rainy season in Gap; up to and including Easter Sunday it has been raining cats and dogs, making it very difficult to get to church. Nevertheless, the church was fairly crowded and it was to these kind people that I gave my last sermon at Vespers on Easter Sunday, after having had dinner with Bishop Berthet.

That night the wind shifted to the north and by Monday morning we had some very beautiful weather. Although the town was under a blanket of snow, the snow melted quickly. The mountains, however, remained thickly coated. I left the Alps, then, while they were in all their glory, pure white against a clear blue sky. The trip from Gap to Marseilles is very pretty, but long: I left at 11:30 a.m. and arrived at 8 p.m. There were many people travelling that day but we weren't slowed down too much. Although it is a little barren, I liked the Sisteron region very much, with its small towns whose colors blended with the grayish-red rocks in the background. The Durance was swollen by the spring rains; but in the valley, almond trees were gently blooming. After leaving Mirabeau, the countryside becomes more rugged as you get closer to Aix; I thought I was thirteen again when I saw the slopes covered with cysts and oak kermes. I hardly even saw the house of the Little Sisters; it was dark by the time we left the station. I didn't see much of Marseilles either, since I left at 8 a.m. on Tuesday. Since I did not know anything about the region around Nîmes, I found the trip very interesting. The most beautiful part was between Montpellier and Cette, where the train goes through some small vineyards with rocky hills on one side and the sea or lagoons on the other. There are really too many vineyards near Narbonne. A few miles down it lets up a bit and you pass nearby mountains that are fairly high. Carcassonne is enchanting; but I saw it under a gray sky and not flooded with sunlight as it is on the travel posters of the P. O.[1]

In Toulouse I had hardly stepped off the train when I headed for the museum and was most cordially greeted by M. Cartailhac, an eminent scholar of pre-history, who did me the honor of showing me a countless number of flints, stones, carved bones, etc., and also the collection of fossils from Quercy. I didn't find the fossils from Quercy very interesting at all; but on the other hand I should have corrected half the labels on the species. I'm especially depending on Montauban, where I'll be tonight at two o'clock.

This morning I'm going to see a little of Toulouse; M. Cartailhac has already shown me some of the sights. The town is

1. Railroad between Paris and Orleans.

very lively; it reminds me of the time we passed through here with Mother and Olivier in 1898. I can't tell yet when I will be returning to Auvergne: but it won't be before the end of next week. I will arrive by way of Brive. Send me the address of Jean Teilhard, if you know it.

All my love and prayers.

Pierre

17

Dear Father and Mother,

I've just returned here (quite safely) and have once again been caught up in this hectic Parisian life which has prevented me from writing you as quickly as I would have wished. It was certainly wonderful to spend two days with you. As usual, it did me a lot of good, even if it was for only a short time.

Since my return to Vieux-Colombier, nothing much has happened; I'm back at the Museum where I'm working on an article which looks like it will take forever to finish; as for my courses, I have fewer than last semester. Sunday I had a happy reunion with my little glassmakers and they were glad to see me. Forty days was enough time for the station at Bourget to be remodelled. They've put in four tracks to handle the Northern Express which doesn't go through Chantilly any more. Sunday morning I found some ice in the courtyard of the factory and saw that the chestnuts, which are usually early, were already ripening on the Blvd. St. Germain. I hope that Puy-de-Dôme will not have frozen over too much.

I received Olivier's letter yesterday, which was very enjoyable, but since it was dated March 4 it doesn't really tell me what he's doing right now. He was complaining about the number of dances and came to the conclusion that life in Santa-Rosalia isn't very different from that in Maringues!

Adieu, dear Father and Mother. My love to you and prayers to all of you at home.

Pierre

18

Dear Father and Mother,

This is just a note to let you know that I'm going on a short trip and will postpone my fortnightly letter until the end of next week. I've decided to go on a geological expedition (with the Institut Catholique) which starts tomorrow and will last until Wednesday (April 30); we will concentrate on the areas around Caën to Bayeux. It's a truly classical section and it's a shame not to know anything about it. I'll write you when I get back and tell you all about it.

Everything is just fine here. After a lot of rain, we've had two very hot days. Today, it's very overcast.

I'm happy to know you are in Sarcenat; it's there that you are most at home and at ease.

I'll write soon. My love and prayers to all.

Pierre

19

Dear Father and Mother,

   I just got back to Paris on Thursday at midnight, —which explains why I didn't write like I said—, after an excellent trip.
   In spite of the fact that it was spent mostly in looking at rocks, here are a few of the details.
   We left at four o'clock last Saturday, which was a beautiful day; our first stop was at Argence, a small hole between Lisieux and Caën, where we went to see the open pits of a huge clay brick-field (Callovian, if that's of any interest to Gabriel or Joseph); the harvest of ammonite fossils was very fruitful and loaded us down quite a bit; it was with these first treasures that we arrived in Caën, our prime concern. I left town regularly every morning about eight o'clock and never returned before dark. I scarcely even saw the town itself. Father will probably think, quite correctly, that it was very cruel. But I did have time to see that the place is quite easygoing and picturesque. The way some of the houses jut out onto the narrow streets you would think you were in Canterbury. It also has a number of old

and pretty churches, along with some quaint stores. The town has something for everyone. It's very old and peaceful and at the same time very lively and up to date. I don't have to tell you about the wonderful cider of this area—and how much they drink of it. . . . We stayed at a family hotel and my little room was across from a spiral staircase in a tower which, I think, gave easy access to the rue Pascal. Caën is famous for its stone. The cathedral of Canterbury was built with it; but it's a bit further than we have explored. Sunday morning we were in Tilly-sur-Seulles (land of visionaries)[1] to see some petrified mollusks in an abundantly green and hilly region; at noon we were in Bayeux, near the well-known cathedral, which is even more majestic when you see the small town that has built it. As is only just, we did come to see some *"bajocien"* stones which gave us some wonderful fossils. Notre Dame des Champs will benefit in part from these findings. Toward four o'clock we reached Port-en-Bessin, a pretty little spot without villas or a casino. It seems like the only inhabitants of the town are clean-shaven and jolly fishermen; this absence of civilization is evidently due to the rocky coasts which are completely unfit for swimming. That day we returned to Caën at 9:30 in the evening.

Monday we took a trip to May, a little south of Caën in a very interesting place, where some Jurassic stones were lying flat on some primeval cliffs—from an ancient sea on some old mountains. The terrain is rather hilly and in some places it is

1. A small market town of Calvados, the center of the "Work of Mercy" founded by the enlightened Pierre Vintras (1807–1875) and condemned by Gregory XVI in 1843. After 1843, Vintras organized his sect into a church, with some priests that he ordained "pontiffs." Maurice Barres based his novel *La Colline inspirée* on this epoch as it appeared in the issues of the *Revue hebdomadaire*.

covered by a carpet of flowering furze which gives off a pleasant fragrance. The banks of the Orne and its tributaries are very pretty at this point; we followed a river (the Laize) for a long time. The shores were heavy with sandstone and marble and at times the banks disappeared in the thick undergrowth. In May there are some large quarries of sandstone, used for paving streets (where we collected some sea fossils here and there)— and also an iron mine. You must have heard about the iron ore from Normandy. The papers talk about it from time to time on account of the Germans monopolizing it. The mine is magnificent and inexhaustible, forming a perfectly marked bed (Silurian) that the samples have found to be very deep. The dust from the ore is blood red and gives the mine's entrance a very strange appearance; it doesn't look like much; a horizontal gallery, on the same level as the Orne, opening onto a wooded hill.

Tuesday we returned to the sea, at Lion-sur-Mer, near Ouistreham. There are rather too many villas in that area, but still we were able to find a good number of fossils in a Bathonian which forms a ridiculously low cliff. From Caën to the sea the country is very pretty: we skirted around the maritime canal, where a huge shipment of ore (German!) was going through, into a grassy meadow, lined with some beautiful trees. There are also beautiful castles all over Normandy. That night a terrible storm unfortunately ruined the weather for the next day. That day, Wednesday, we first stopped at Villers-sur-Mer and Trouville. The first place is famous for its ammonites (Jurassic) which were pyritized in the clay along the sea shore. We found some, but under a drizzle that lasted until six o'clock that evening. The clay cliffs were black with mud and reminded me of the worst days in Hastings. From Trouville we took the boat to Havre

(Trouville is a cluster of villas and casinos, as you would probably suppose, and where a cup of tea costs one franc during the prime season). The sun came out for a while and shone on the water. The crossing (an hour) was pretty good, except that someone took my umbrella. When we arrived, I was able to pick out the four smoke-stacks of the *France* and imagined that Yéyé left on it. Fortunately, Thursday was a beautiful day; in the morning we went down to the bottom of the majestic cliffs of the Hève; that night we visited the chalk deposits in Rouen, which seemed to be a very nice city in spite of the overabundance of factories smoking away on the left bank. I didn't visit any churches; the entire view of the city is a beautiful sight. I was happy to spend the three days before the feast of Joan of Arc there.

You see we didn't waste our time. I'm back working at the Museum again, but I'll leave tonight and go to Bourget to see young Vaure and his friends. I imagine that tomorrow Paris will be magnificent.

This morning I received Mother's letter. I've also received Father's and Guiguite's. I really wish Guiguite had some more free time. My best to Gabriel. Love to all.

Pierre

20

Dear Father and Mother,

Let me begin by assuring you that I have received the money order for both the umbrella and the book *Villatte des Prugnes*. The first should make Mother happy and the second is very interesting. Thank you for them both. Father's last letter arrived this morning and I was distressed to hear of Guiguite's renewed suffering. I will remember her and you in a special Mass. God is a good Master and He knows His own will best. Let's pray that this new crisis doesn't last too long.

I wrote my last letter after I had returned from Normandy; two days later Paris celebrated the feast of Joan of Arc with tremendous dignity in spite of the foul weather. You've probably read about it in the papers. Sitting on the stone base of a wrought-iron fence, I was able to see the rows of paraders and floats. The group from the Action Française was by far the best organized and performed extremely well; in second place I have to mention the squad of little gymnasts from Michaud. This has certainly been a week of big events: because I had chosen Thursday to make an overdue visit to Uncle Georges and my aunt, up near the Invalides I ran into a review (in honor of Alphonsus XIII)[1] just then breaking up; I almost didn't reach my destination, for I saw (for the first time in my life!) some cuirassiers and dragoons filing by in the bright sunlight. In the morning I had been asked to assist with the first communions at Notre Dame des Champs, along with several cloaked canons. The ceremony was very nice; the father of one of the "little ones," who was escorting the first communicants dressed in white with a lily in their hands, sobbed with emotion. That night during the sermons the little boy I just spoke of, or one of his classmates, fell sound asleep; but I wasn't there to see it.

I've met Glangeaud; I missed him when he was at the Museum but finally got to see him at the Geological Society, where he explained to us how the Michelin drilling, because of a lack of water, had brought back proof that Côme had erupted at least nine times. Apropos of geology, the description of my plant fossils (from Hastings) has appeared in the journal of the London Geological Society. There's a genre Teilhardia and a species Teilhardi, among others. In paleobotany we have a record of all types of species with bizarre names; at least that's the proof of the great kindness of Professor Seward, the author of the study. I was at Bourget two weeks ago (I go back there day after tomorrow) and found that young Vaure was as astonished as he was delighted to learn he had a compatriot. He has not forgotten Guiguite.

Goodbye, dear Father and Mother. All my love.

Pierre

1. Alphonsus XIII was king of Spain from 1902 to 1931.

21

Dear Father and Mother,

I've just received Mother's letter which says that Guiguite is about the same. When you are away, you always learn about things when they are more or less over; but you, you have had to spend some anxious moments during this new crisis. I think God will reward you for all that.

I'm a bit annoyed with Olivier for not writing regularly; but as far as the risks which the revolution might entail for him, I assure you that I have no such uneasiness.

Gabriel will have told you that I am going to go and "dig" in Spain; I think I'll be leaving towards the 12th and will most assuredly write you from there. Santander is not far; but beyond the Pyrenees the roads are long when travelling: Obermaier told me to telegraph him 48 hours in advance!

As for the usefulness of this trip, it will be a real vacation for me because I'll be roving through some very beautiful country.

The past two weeks have been very boring and this past week was extremely hot. Fortunately, it's been raining since early this evening. Sunday I went to Montreuil; nothing has changed at all. It was a demonstration day in Pré-St.-Gervais; aside from two or three eglantines, there was nothing to give a suspicion of it. While the socialists were entertaining the federates, the rest of us were remembering those who had been shot down on the rue Haxo, which is a great testimony to the PP. de Paris. I didn't have time to go to rue Haxo, but I did say Mass in the chapel of the rue de Sèvres, where the bodies had been taken. At this time the chapel is being used as a show place for church ornaments, supplied by the work of the missions. The exhibit makes this lonely place a bit more pleasant.

Gabriel must also have told you that I gave a lecture on the subject of evolution before the teaching staff of Notre Dame des Champs; I'm going to speak again on Tuesday about a related subject.

Tonight, as usual, I'm going to Bourget; because of the weather we've been having lately, the poor kids didn't need their crucibles to keep warm.

Goodbye for now. My love to all.

Pierre

22

[*San Sebastián, June 6, 1913*]

Dear Father and Mother,

Except for the fact that it's cloudy and there isn't a yacht in sight, San Sebastián is a very pretty place and is quite exotic. I took a very good trip during which I was able to determine the damage done by the Adour. Tomorrow I start out for stony Spain, with a practically non-existent command of the language. Fortunately, Obermaier will be there if I should need him. I spent one afternoon here; aside from the seaport there's another old town, with sculptured hotels and old somber churches, overloaded with ornaments but nonetheless majestic. And then there is that mighty ocean which shatters its green waves against the rocks from which swarthy Basques fish for some fairly good-sized catches.

Many people on the balconies.

I'll write you when I finally get to where I'm going.

Pierre

23

Dear Father and Mother,

Since I was imprudent enough not to write you from Santander, and since it will be 11 a.m. tomorrow before my letter
goes out, that means you won't get this until Tuesday at the
earliest. You'll think I've been lost somewhere in Biscaye! But
don't worry. I've finally arrived and will tell you about my
wanderings, namely, about a ravishing little village, the same
size as Orcines, built at the foot of some fair-sized mountains
and by a river which is rushing past my window with a great
speed not more than fifty feet away.

You can see what it's like from the picture I've enclosed (and
which you asked me to take); like all pictures taken from great
heights, it flattens out the background. Aside from that, you
can see the torrent, the high mountains to the south, the site
of the excavations (marked with an X, on the mountain to the
right; you can see the cone of the scree fairly well). The "hotel"
is out of sight in the lower left corner; the building itself is
square and is near a bridge (romanesque and very artistic), the

Puente Viesgo (Old Bridge) is a bath house; there are natural hot springs here that attract people from all over, starting from June 15. Because of this, several houses are converted into hotels. By doing this the area's natural beauty isn't destroyed. The one where I am staying is a long shanty, an old house with long corridors and monastic-like rooms on either side. But they are extremely clean and well-kept, which, it seems, is strange for Spain. There are five of us: an Austrian (Dr. Obermaier), an Alsatian (his assistant), an Englishman (Burkitt, a Cambridge professor's son, very charming), a Yankee (an expert on Pre-Colombian civilization), —and me. It seems (for I've just come) that they are a good group; I say this only from what I've already seen. I'd like to start working right away; but I must be patient until Monday.

Yesterday my trip was good but very long. To get here you must take a small train that speeds along an incredibly winding route. On leaving San Sebastián, you pass through two or three small Basque ports, quite romantic, nestled in some coves, then on through high massive mountains, partly covered by very beautiful forests of oak and chestnut, more often by huge green oak trees. On the plains you begin to see a species of purple orchid with very large petals which has intrigued me for two days, because you can see them everywhere and I won't be able to pick any until tomorrow. There was a three-hour stop in Bilbao; there, as in St. Sebastián and Santander, the railroad station is separate, apparently to extract a few more pesetas from the poor travelers. The weather, which had been bad, changed, and it was under a sunny sky that I roamed through narrow streets, bordered by innumerable balconies (always covered with linen put out to dry); a group of roving musicians played some very Spanish tunes on flutes and guitars which I could have listened to forever. The two churches I visited seemed exactly the same: very somber, very high, and very ornate. All the statues are quite pretty and rather expressive. The clock-towers in this region are inevitably square towers topped by a round dome; around the clock is a great deal of sculpture. As for the inhabitants, their reputation for moral and physical health is evident everywhere; it shines through their large, smiling faces, topped off with a small beret. I'm not as impressed with the soldiers; when I see them, I always think I'm looking at one of those horrible caricatures of Alphon. XIII you see in the papers. Their bizarre polished helmets seem to have a bad effect on me.

From Bilbao to Santander the trip is very beautiful; you continue to cross great mountains, often wooded, and the tract is so narrow that you would think you are rolling along on a hollow road; at one place there were cows almost standing on the tracks. The sky cleared and it was as beautiful as it is today. I'm in the nicest part of Spain; the moisture coming off the gulf of Gascony condenses to a great extent on the mountains— to the detriment of the regions further south. It also seems that this isn't as rugged a region; yesterday, at the hotel, a French-man who works for the mines and does a lot of travelling told me there was a village in the Sierra Morena which was 30 miles from any other civilization! This whole area is very rich in mines, especially iron mines. The ore seems to be deposited on some mountains by dripping into the limestone cracks and gives the stone a marbleized effect: in some spots the only things left are fantastic harrows, like a forest of menhirs. Transporting the material is the hard part; in some places little wagons and cable cars carry it across valleys.

Santander is a pretty town but too small; the bay is magnificent and has a beautiful panorama of mountains around it; it eventually flows into lakes, which makes me doubt its depth. At the spot where the bay rejoins the ocean the townsmen built a magnificent palace which they gave to the king in order to get him and his court to come down to San Sebastián and spend some time. Many of the freighters are filled with iron ore but there are no pleasure boats. It's much better than Bilbao where the ships arrive on the river, —exactly like they do in Caën (except here it is mostly English ships that take the iron). On the quay in Santander there's a small but well-stocked aquarium whose caretaker, when he wants to be "friendly," bothers the fish by poking them with a hook: when he manages to disturb a ray, that's still all right, but when he makes the polyps and *tubicoles* curl up or the star fish dance, it's absolutely hysterical.

I'll write you in a few days and give you my impression of the excavation. I'm becoming more and more convinced of the chance to do some research here; conditions both scientific and personal—and, I would add, pleasurable—are really exceptional. Would you believe it?

There's a chapel in the house (because of the bathers) and permission to say Mass has just come through for this evening! If it hadn't been for this providential opportunity, I really think we would have had to miss more than one Mass; and I owe the chance to Mother.

Adieu! All my love and prayers.

Pierre

82

24

[Puente-Viesgo, June 16, 1913]

Dear Father and Mother,

Ten days have already flown by. It just seems like it was only yesterday that I arrived. Everything seems to be piling up and I thought I'd bring you up to date right away as to what's happened since my last letter. Basically, I've been roaming the countryside looking at dirt and stones. Early this morning, about eight, we climbed up to the cavern wearing the right clothes, of course, and stayed there until six—out in the fresh air and beautiful sunlight and taking advantage of a spectacular view. We didn't find anything extraordinary; the deposits, though there were more of them, were the same as last year's; but even this was very interesting because it's the best remains of quaternary dwellings yet found. Presently, a good part of the cavern's hall (only section that was used as a dwelling) has been cleared away, but the work takes a long time. The height of the deposits is around 50 feet and this year they've unearthed a section more than 260 sq. feet. We are on the third level next to the last lived in (there are twelve in all), that is, in the deepest and most interesting section. You can see very distinctly (often separated by chalk deposits which can be 60 inches thick and which must be dynamited) the carbon layers, fossilized bone splinters, teeth, and bones. These beds are painstakingly scraped and all the objects are carefully sorted. This week the remains we dug up included a great amount of deer, but also some rhinoceros, horse, ibex, bear, lion, hyena, —but unfortunately none of man. Hand-carved tools are also found very frequently. The end of the cave's hallway opens into a real grotto, about 650 feet long, sufficiently divided and filled with stalactites. It's there and often in the most remote corners that you find drawings and paintings from different epochs. There's an elephant, and also some does, and some horses; what is even more interesting is one wall covered with pictures of hands. They must have put their left hand against the rock, then drawn around it with ochre (the hands are white on a red background). Very good meditation material can be found by looking at these vestiges of pre-historic man; I like to look at it alone, in an absolute silence, disturbed only by the drops falling off the stalactites. Right near Castillo there is another grotto, narrower and yet more mysterious; I still don't know it very well.

The best of the quaternary paintings is a two-hour drive from here, by the seacoast, in Altamira, I went there on Thursday. The grotto was nothing to look at from the outside; just a little hole in the midst of green furze and meadows filled with orchids. It had been completely sealed off (which kept the paintings intact) and was found by accident during a mining operation. To say nothing of the main chamber which contained a number of animal drawings, there were plenty of bear tracks on the stalagmites or even in the soft clay. I found a marvellous sight in one section where the roof is covered with magnificent bison, painted in three colors (red, yellow, and black) and with an extraordinary degree of clarity and expression. There were nine of them, all very well preserved, each about seven feet long. For three of them the artists utilized the natural curve of the rock and to keep the bison in these curves, they painted them in some unbelievably bold positions; I especially liked the one which was pictured in the midst of a charge and whose eyes were livid with rage. When you think that these were drawn during an age when Egyptian culture was surely non-existent, you are completely amazed. But you must also try to discover what these paintings meant to their primitive creators, and this is quite disturbing. I must confess I didn't go back there again.

In order to go to Altamira you must stop at Santillane, which must be the most curious of all the little Spanish towns you could imagine. In the past, when the Moors occupied Spain, it was the (one of the? . . .) capital of the northern provinces which succeeded in resisting all attacks. It then became the retreat of the noble hidalgos. Now it's almost a ghost town, about as big as Vialle, but where nearly every house is an ancient casa of a noble Spaniard (more or less transformed into a stable). On each façade, between the two narrow windows of the second floor, under the balcony (which is surmounted by large wooden half-columns framing the third floor) you can see enormous escutcheons covered with complicated coats of arms and supported by sculpted dragons lacking both taste and moderation. The church, romanesque, and which surely goes back mainly to the tenth century, must be an archeologist's dream. A cloister still remains, whose cornices represent some scenes of the struggle against Islam, —most frequently an armored knight plunging his spear into a dragon. I hope to get some pictures. And Santillane isn't even mentioned in the Baedeker.

It's a real shame that no one in Spain cares enough to save this relic.

I tried to collect a few insects from the grottos but I've only seen a few so far: only a small reddish-brown moth, some galley-worms and some *scolopendra*.

Yesterday, Sunday, we visited some English friends. They are engineers in the iron mines. We were treated royally in a very pretty house, surrounded by a garden, full of roses, palm trees, and also some Canterbury bells (*Campanula*) and some Veronicas all of which remind one of England. After a cigar, we played croquet (the latest thing). The lady of the house paints flowers in a truly intriguing fashion; she assured me that the big purple orchid that I liked so much is *O. militaris,* but she must be mistaken. It must be something like a Serapias. I'm going to try and send one of the flowers in this envelope.

I've noted with satisfaction that I'm having less trouble with my English; it seems that I understand it better now that I've left Hastings!

Well, I must leave to go to the grotto.[1] It would amuse you to see me wearing alparagates, or the native sandals. I forgot to tell Father that three vultures, probably griffons, paid us a visit in Castillo, probably attracted by some dead cattle in the mountains. One of them stopped very close to us; you could see the movements of its long nude neck quite distinctly.

1. See H. Breuil, H. Obermaier, and H. Alcalde del Rio, "La Pasiega, a Puente-Viesgo (Santander)," in *l'Anthropologie*, t. 27, p. 585.

Excuse my handwriting, but the constant lifting of stones makes it difficult for me to hold a pen.

Adieu. My love to all. I've received all your letters.

Pierre

I think I'll be staying here till the first few days in July.

25

Puente-Viesgo, June 30, 1913

Dear Father and Mother,

My stay here is coming to an end; I plan on leaving Wednesday; Thursday I'll be in Lourdes, Friday night in Toulouse, Saturday night in Vieux-Colombier. That's the reason I have to leave, for I've been very happy here; the more you work on the layers the less you learn about the excavations: it's too bad I must go at this precise time. Last week was spent, like the others, in the cavern, except for a very beautiful trip to the grotto of Pindal, located on the seashore, to the west of Santander on the outskirts of the province of Oviedo. The grotto itself is very beautiful, about 1200 feet long, exceptionally high and clean, hung with an abundant fringe of stalactites bristling from the ceiling or splashing into large lacy cloths. Abbe Breuil himself did us the honor of describing the paleolithic drawings, which included among others an elephant and a beautiful fish; afterwards, he and I went looking for insects and I found my first

PIERRE TEILHARD DE CHARDIN

real mosquitos (I told Gabriel about them in my last letter, according to M. Alluand (of the Duvalins?)).

One of the really beautiful sights of the day was the ocean, crystal clear and ever so quiet. As far as you could see, from east to west, there were mounds of little pointed rocks on the green waters; there were also the green oaks which made you think you were in Brittany or England; Burkitt felt nostalgia for Scotland immediately. Unfortunately, clouds were perched on the mountains. Otherwise, this magnificent view would have been completed by the glaciers of the Picos d'Europa which are not more than 40 miles from the coast; but we had to content ourselves with a view of the sea. We profited by having Breuil along with us when we saw the drawings of Castillo and the neighboring caves.[1] He showed us all of them. Yesterday he left for the Picos with M. Alluand who is driving there to look for some special Carabidae near the snow line. M. Alluand seems to be a charming man, bubbling over with good health and entomological enthusiasm. He and his wife have made I don't know how many trips to Madagascar and Uganda, which gives them the chance to tell us some beautiful tales; they are from the Creuse region.

I still don't know what I'll be doing in August or September; that will be decided when I return to Paris, where I'll most likely be staying for the rest of July. I'll write you at the beginning of the next week.[2]

1. See H. Breuil and H. Obermaier, "Fouilles de l'Institut de Paleontologie humaine a la grotte de Castillo," in *l'Anthropologie* t. 23 (1913), p. 601 ff.
2. For some details on the expedition in his last four letters see Cl. Cuénot, *op. cit.*, pp. 35–36.

Goodbye for now, All my love to you, Guiguite, and the boys. I don't have to tell you that I'll be thinking of you when I'm in Lourdes.

Pierre

26

Dear Father and Mother,

As usual, every time I come back to Paris, and even more so this time, I'm thrown into this whirlpool of activity and scarcely can find the time to write. You can see I've arrived safe and sound; the return from Puente Viesgo—which was preceded by a farewell party at the Vallesoletana hotel—was very good. First of all, I noticed that the "express" between Santander-Bilbao was able to make everyone as seasick as if they were on a steamboat in rough weather. Two passengers were even hanging out the door and a third nearly joined them. Aside from this, the weather and scenery were wonderful. In Lourdes I met pilgrims from St. Brieuc and Madrid; with all that's going on, it's very difficult to pray quietly in the grotto; on the other hand, you can see the others praying and the devotion of the stretcher-bearers, which struck me more than all the rest. I saw the procession of the Blessed Sacrament which surely is a moving ceremony, after which Dr. Boissarie took me into the office of verification where a few interesting "improvements" are on file, but no definite cures except one, perhaps. Friday morning I said Mass in the Basilica and remembered all of you. From there I immediately left for Montauban, which I found quite pleasant; the keys of the museum were waiting for me so that I could quickly make up any notes I was missing. And then I returned here Saturday night. I really liked the ride between Brive and Limoges and felt relatively close to Sarcenat.

I hope Victor is now happily settled in his new position. I'm going to try, as Father asked me, to enter his name in the Postes. Here all you see are people taking exams; yesterday on the bus a candidate at some big school needed a confidant so badly that he confided his hopes to the ticket agent! Speaking of exams, how is Gonzague doing with his law studies? Everyone asks me about Guiguite. I do wish her the best, and soon.

Adieu, Father and Mother. My love to all at Sarcenat.

Pierre

Thanks to Mother for her letter, which I found when I arrived.

27

Paris, July 27, 1913

Dear Father and Mother,

I'm afraid that it's been almost three weeks since my last letter . . .

Since I've returned from Spain I've been extremely busy; I'm trying to finish up my research work by October and I had to take about 100 pictures—all of which are not exactly *chefs-d'oeuvre*. But I'm nearly finished. I leave Paris on August 1. Friday night I'll be in Canterbury (Hales Place, Canterbury, Kent) where I think I'll be until the 8th and from there I go on to Hastings. I will make my retreat at Ore Place from the 15th to the 24th; in the beginning of September I'll be going to Jersey to do a little excavating. I'll be back at Vieux-Colombier by the 1st of October.

Around the 10th of July I went to Uncle Georges' for dinner and was almost late, thanks to some Madagascan and Tonkinese soldiers who were marching along the same boulevard as my trolley; I was as welcome as ever and in true Auvergne style. I also said my goodbyes to the Cirices before they left on their vacation; I was even invited to the award-giving night at Notre Dame des Champs and crowned the glorious Cecilia.

I'm writing during a terrible storm that is raging in our section of Paris; there's a little hail and a lot of rain; I hope this won't delay the rainy season.

I love you all; my next letter won't be so long in coming.

Pierre

28

Canterbury, August 6, 1913

Dear Father and Mother,

Sunday I received Mother's letter that gave me the good news about Guiguite and the day before yesterday I received Fran-çoise's announcement.[1] I was very happy about Guiguite, natu-rally, and after reading Françoise's note over, I liked it very much. I would think you would have sent one to Father Froc.

I'm writing you from Canterbury, a place I hardly knew be-fore, having spent only an occasional afternoon there, but after fourteen months I now know it inside out.[2] I arrived after an excellent trip, although a little rough; despite the clear sky, the Channel was extremely windy and rough right from the jetty at the Boulogne crossing. It was a total disaster for the countless tourists who swarm all over the place. Thanks to the train from

1. Françoise Teilhard de Chardin, Little Sister of the Poor (Cler-mont-Ferrand, 1913). These *Souvenirs* gathered by his sister Marguerite-Marie have been reproduced almost entirely in the biography of *Soeur Marie-Alberic du Sacre-Coeur*. See *Letters from Egypt* (New York, 1966), letter 8.
2. He spent his "Third Year" there. See letter 58, note.

Etlam valley, you arrive here faster than to Hastings. Along the way I renewed my acquaintance with the sheep and calves. There I found the peace of a large park, two-thirds wooded with magnificent trees, and which you might almost find too beautiful if you could only forget that it was given primarily to a college. Rabbits abound, as well as squirrels, thrushes, wood pigeons, and of course robins. And if you look precisely at the proper angle you have a very pleasing view of the towers of the cathedral. I arrived Friday night. The next day, at the same time, I picked up Bob at the station and he stayed here until Sunday night. Sunday morning we explored the town extensively—or as well as we could on a day when everything is closed. The streets are extraordinarily alive with excitement, especially High Street (the only main thoroughfare) because this is the annual Cricket Week. Innumerable cars bring in a colorful, motley crowd, and there is the spectacle of rows of little red and yellow flames festooning the houses on either side of the street. We heard the first psalms of the office in the cathedral, having arrived early enough to see the mace-bearers and the children of the choir, dressed in purple cassocks and high white collars, preceding the very gentlemanly canon who sprinkled holy water. From there we went to St. Martin's, a small and modest chapel surrounded by yew-trees, whose Roman foundations are probably the remains of the first Catholic church in England. In the end we went to see the "Invicta," one of the first locomotives of Stephenson, which decorates a small square along the old ramparts, after having made the run between Canterbury-Whitstable. We finished the evening resting under some trees in a pleasant spot of the park.

In order not to neglect my geology, yesterday I took a long-

planned trip to Sheppey. Sheppey is an island, a little more surrounded by water than Thanet, very close to here, but which
you can reach only by way of the Queenboro line; its whole
southern portion is totally flat and swampy but towards the
north the land picks up and along the estuary of Tamise is a
clay cliff about 60 feet high in the middle, noted for its fossils
(according to Gabriel and Joseph, it is London clay, inferior
Eocene). As a matter of fact, I brought back some palm tree
seeds, several sea fossils, and two admirable small crabs, one of
which looks like it was about to snap its pincers. The countryside
is very green and has an excellent view of Tamise; to the west
the cruisers and battleships lined up in the port of Catham; you
could also see a number of steamships. There was also a hydro-
plane opposite us, making a horrible noise and leaving a huge
wake in its path. To the east you could follow the coast up to
Margate.

In spite of the charms of Canterbury I leave the day after
tomorrow but will only be in Hastings Sunday or Monday. I'm
going to stop in Lewes for 48 hours (near New Haven) and
will stay with my friend Dawson to search the gravel pits where
they found the Sussex Man last year.[3] The worst part will be
trying to remember all my English. And so, I'll arrive at Ore
a few days before the 15th; that night I begin my retreat. I'll
write you from there.

My love and prayers to all.

                                              Pierre

3. Up to the present Teilhard had not taken part in any of Dawson's
discoveries, and he trusts him.

29

Ore Place, Hastings, August 15, 1913

Dear Father and Mother,

Well, I'm back at Hastings and using this very familiar type of stationery again. I'm only half used to finding myself here again, not as a student but as a "theologian." I arrived here Monday night after an excellent stay in Lewes with my friend Dawson. I told you once before that he lives in a very pretty villa, covered with ivy and surrounded with flowers and located within the very walls of the old castle of Lewes. I was received there in true English fashion like an old friend; they took care of my every whim and for three days I lived in the purest comfort of this most enjoyable of homes. Most of the time we spent digging in Uckfield in the gravel pits of Piltdown; I went on Friday afternoon, all day Saturday, and Sunday afternoon. This type of research is completely "exciting"; unfortunately, we didn't find too much this time: just a small fragment of a nose (?). At least the weather was beautiful. Piltdown is a very beautiful corner of Sussex, with many trees, near a "golf course," and it has a very beautiful park which you have to go through to get to Uckfield. During the three days, Dr. Woodward, from the British Museum, worked with us.

Mr. Dawson's son was visiting him, too. He is an officer in a Camel corps and is stationed in Sudan; a very nice young man; he showed me a number of pictures, especially a few of some antelope he had killed. On Sunday morning I helped Mrs. Dawson cut some sweet peas and make up a few bouquets; it reminded me of when I was in Santander and of Mrs. Bettie whose garden I had also enjoyed. Mother would have laughed if she had seen me out there. Mrs. Dawson explained the aesthetical effects produced in the bouquets by a type of *stellaria* (?), a very fine (*Gipsofila?* . . .) and she suggested that I send you a root (I told her that you liked flowers).

That Sunday I said Mass in a small church in Lewes for a very fine group, most of whom came from London; Sussex doesn't have many Catholics, except maybe Brighton. Monday I went to London with Mr. Dawson and Dr. Woodward to attend an exhibition of the remains from Piltdown, held by the Congress of medical anatomists (among them I found many I had known from the Museum). At the second session, which I could not attend, having taken the train for Hastings, Dr. Woodward was very much criticized by a certain Professor Keith who wants (and rightly so, I believe) to have the skull reassembled in a new way.

In my opinion, all these reconstructions aren't of much interest and don't add any certainty about it; other pieces have to be found.[1]

Tonight, then, I begin my retreat; I won't forget to pray for

1. See letter 28.

you this week and will write you when it's over. I plan on staying at Ore until the 4th or 5th of September.

Olivier's request for books is going to be a little difficult to supply because of his generality; but I'll try to find some recent books that are noteworthy; in the meantime, Gabriel could perhaps send him the *Revue Générale des Sciences*. I certainly don't dislike all tertiary fossils, at the most just shark's teeth; I'll write Olivier to see what he finds.

Is M. de Morgan, who is now on vacation in Royat, a relative of the famous explorer from Egypt and Persia?[2]

Adieu, Father and Mother. All my love to you, Guiguite, and the boys.

Pierre

2. Jacques de Morgan, Orientalist and numismatist. He had published some *Recherches sur les origines de l'Egypte,* then some memoires on *la Delegation du ministere de l'Instruction publique en Perse,* and in 1909 a synthesis on *les Anciennes Civilisations.* In 1921 he will publish *l'Humanite prehistorique* and in 1925–1927 *la Prehistoire orientale.*

30

Ore Place, August 29, 1913

Dear Father and Mother,

I must thank you for your letter and Guiguite's which arrived at the close of my retreat; mine will take a little longer, but due to the lack of news and time it won't be too long; however unlikely it may seem, I'm having trouble trying to fill all I wanted to do into my schedule here at Hastings, and must even drop a few plans, namely, a visit to certain quarries which would have been the same for me as Faumagny was for Father and my brothers last November. I've had to be satisfied with going back to the cliffs where I've brought back a very beautiful (but hardly a rare species) fish. Retreat ended Sunday with ordination which was exactly the same as it was two years ago. The weather was beautiful but the parents must have had to put up with a stormy sea the day before. You can be sure that the ceremony brought back many and fond memories to which you weren't exactly a stranger.

This year we couldn't get into Ashburnham; the park is now closed to us; after several inquiries, all of which proved fruitless,

I think I can say that Lady Catherine is not yet at Sacre-Coeur. They even told me in Lewes that she is now on a world tour, at her father's "suggestion"!

Tomorrow, Saturday, I'm going back to Lewes for the day to see an excavation, of course. On my way back to Hastings I have to pick up Bob and bring him back to Ore Place where he'll stay until Sunday. I'll find out tomorrow exactly what my schedule will be for next week; in any case, don't write me here anymore, but at "Maison St. Louis, St. Helier, Jersey, *Iles Normandes*." I think I'll be there Saturday or Sunday.

Who would have thought that Planchard's daughter was at Ashford! As far as Holy Child[1] is concerned, I don't have very many dealings over there; I only know that it's a rather stylish house and its location, on top of a hill that separates Hastings from St. Leonard, is just beautiful. From Ore Place you can see the chapel and the pension which looks out on the sea.

I wish you a beautiful opening Sunday in Chardin;[2] It's too bad there aren't any deer left in Villeneuve, but it's a pretty name just the same. The other day, on the cliffs, I shot some very beautiful pheasants, amidst some gorgeous scenery.

I'm anxiously following, as you are, what's happening in Mexico; I don't see anything for Olivier to worry about; except maybe the hot weather.

Adieu, dear Father and Mother. My love to you all. I urge Gabriel to go on working.

Pierre

1. A pension held by the religious of the "Infant Jesus."
2. A hunt in the large grounds of Chardin, in Villeneuve-les-Cerfs (Puy-de-Dôme), which belong to the Teilhard de Chardin family.

31

Ipswich, Friday

I leave tomorrow for Jersey; from there I'll write you a longer letter. Everything is fine.

My love to all.

Pierre

32

Dear Father and Mother,

I'm writing you with this very familiar view of St. Helier before my eyes, the two clock towers of Fort Elizabeth, Point Noirmont, which guards the bay, and in the foreground Waiverley Terrace. I arrived here Sunday morning after a very busy though interesting week, which I must tell you about. First of all, Saturday, the 30th, the day after I wrote you (I think), I went to Lewes to have breakfast at Castle Lodge. Afterwards Mr. Dawson and I left to go digging in Uckfield along with Dr. Woodward[1]; among the workers I'll have to include a "pet goose" who never left us alone while we were digging. At times he was gentle, at others cantankerous towards us, but he was always ferocious towards the passers-by. This time we were lucky: in the earth dug up from previous excavations and now washed by rain I found the canine tooth from the jaw of the famous Piltdown Man, —an important piece of evidence for Dr. Woodward's reconstruction plan: it was a very exciting experience! Imagine,

1. See letters 28 and 29.

it was the last excavation of the season![2] And so it was with a light heart that I returned to Hastings, where I had to pick up Bob; amidst the hubbub of a busy railroad station on a weekend, we missed each other: Bob finally managed to make his way to Ore Place around nine o'clock that night. We spent a wonderful Sunday together, even though it rained nearly all day; we even had time for a visit to the cliffs. I was planning to see Bob again in London; but I haven't had the time. I arrived in London on Tuesday morning (Sept. 25), and had the honor of staying with Dr. Woodward who was most hospitable. Even his wife, who was at the seashore, was anxious to know if I was *properly fed*— and I must say that everything was superb. He had me write my name on a piece of cloth covered with the signatures of many geological celebrities, and spent an enjoyable evening *tête à tête* with Woodward, a certain Gregory (from the New York Museum, an important contact), and an ornithologist from the British Museum, Pycraft, whom Father perhaps knows. I did some useful work at the British Museum for two days and then left for Ipswich (Suffolk) where I was anxious to see some

2. Such was the last meeting of Father Teilhard with Charles Dawson and such was his contribution to the discovery of the "Piltdown Man." See our introduction, pp. 9–10. As early as November 28 Teilhard had written to Oakley: "I most sincerely congratulate you on your findings in the case of the Piltdown Man. Anatomically speaking, the 'Eoanthropus' was a species of monster, etc." See R. P. Bergounioux, *La Préhistoire et ses problèmes* (1958), p. 227: "The finding of a human skull, undoubtedly *sapiens,* and what was most likely a monkey's jaw in the same pit really gave the paleontologists a thorny problem. . . . It took 50 years and the most precise techniques and resources to shed any light on the question. The result of this expert evaluation was astonishing and totally confused those too confident anatomists who wanted to combine the skull of a truly prehistoric *homo sapiens* and the mandible of an ape." As to the "method of fluorine" used in this analysis, see *ibid.,* pp. 86–88.

ground that was very important to me. I was met by Mr. Reid Moir and stayed at his home. During the two-day stay he drove me around to all the noteworthy spots. I met a very charming man, Colonel Underwood (who was crazy about silex and had them lying about all over his house), who, as I've been told by everyone, is typically English, very distinguished, and quite witty; I don't think I've ever heard such racy language. He told me that one of his great aunts was the wife of Montalembert. Ipswich is not as smoky as my postcard would have you think; a third of the town is taken up by public parks and the villas are surrounded by large gardens. The countryside is hilly and very green; I've not gotten as far as the sea.

Friday night I returned to London to stay overnight and then went to Jersey, via Weymouth, on Saturday morning. Forgetting that there was no longer any day service from Weymouth in September, I arrived a half day too soon and had to kill time anyway I could. The place is very beautiful; it is near the harbor of Portland and you can see cruisers and dreadnoughts when you've had enough of the cliffs and countryside; I stayed there four years ago when I was on my way back to Hastings from Jersey; this time I excused myself from going to the Portland peninsula, since I could hardly find a place to rest as it was. The crossing was rather rough and I shamefully succumbed to the tortures of seasickness. Around 6 a.m. we were in St. Pierre de Guernsey, in the middle of the archipelago which I knew so well, and arrived in Corbière and Jersey two hours later. Among other things I'll be digging around a fissure on the north coast; I went up there for a first inspection the day before yesterday; it's marvelous and easily accessible; but I doubt I'll find anything worth while.

At the College of Bon-Secours I met Christian Burdo (whose mother I saw before leaving Hastings); he is studying philosophy and he seemed happy to be here again; he had first been assigned to Marneffe. At St. Louis I met Father Bonnet,[3] my own philosophy professor at Mongré, whom I hadn't seen since!

I've received all your letters; I'm sorry that you are all alone during vacation time. I'm very happy for Gabriel and was pleased to hear he stayed at Montauban.

I pray that the Blessed Virgin may help Guiguite on Monday; but I don't dare hope too much. Good things usually happen when you least expect them . . .

My love to all, and especially to Guiguite.

In London I offered Mass at Westminster; the interior is still very empty.

You are always in my prayers.

Pierre

3. Father Camille Bonnet (1855–1944) taught philosophy for thirty-five years (at Mongré, Ghazir, Alexandria, Jersey) and theology for eighteen years (at the University of St. Joseph in Beirut).

33

Dear Father and Mother,

Well, my stay here is quickly drawing to a close; next Friday by 10 p.m. I will be back at 13 de la rue du Vieux Colombier and I must say it will be good to get back: thus I will be in Paris when Victor returns.

The last two weeks have been very restful but I was still kept busy; my free time was spent making notes on the little beasts of Quercy (the transcription is still not finished), and the rest of the time I was in class.

I did get to explore that crevice I had mentioned; it's a hallow grotto by the sea and shows a time when Jersey was on higher ground than now; on the floor of the grotto there is still some gravel left by the sea over the years. The gravel itself contains the remnants of a ruminant (probably washed up by the waves), and it was this that I was really after. Despite the hard work we weren't able to recover much, and although the two horns we found are almost intact, I don't know if we can use them in determining the species of deer. Digging is extremely difficult, especially because the chalk deposits are so hard and because the crevice itself is very narrow; you also have to work with whatever light is available. I did a few other things that were less confining than a cave and the time was well spent. I left with a greater knowledge of Paris—due largely to the efforts of Mr. Manger (Captain (honorary!) of the island troops) who spends eight months of the year on the Blvd. St. Germain studying law and mineralogy. He is very nice and is one of the few "Jersey gentlemen" left from the old days. It is amazing how well he knows the history of the island, the names and background of all the country landlords, and he has a library filled with old books and manuscripts on the subject. In spite of the fact that he barely spoke French, Father would enjoy his conversation. The other day he took me in a chauffeured car, bearing his coat of arms, on some roads that I had never seen before from so noble a position.

For about ten days we've been having quite a few thunder storms, and some have been pretty bad; but in this lucky section the sky is still blue and the rain is starting to give the land its beautiful autumn colors. Father Burdo and I went to see high tide come in around the huge reefs of Seymour tower—like when we used to go fishing years ago; it was a "glorious" evening with all the rocks standing out in red amidst a glossy and pearl-like sea. I don't remember Egypt being as pretty as Jersey.

Adieu. My love and prayers to all; if possible my Mass on the 27th will be for Albéric and the family. Our cry to God will once more be: "Your will be done!"

Pierre

34

My dear little Mother,

I know that I owe Guiguite a few letters, but I'm sure that since today is the feast of Our Lady of the Seven Sorrows she won't mind that this letter is for you. This morning I offered Mass for all your special intentions, my dear, sweet Mother, asking Our Lord through His Blessed Mother to help you better recognize His will and to understand that this suffering when offered up to Him is, indeed, a good. Little by little the years roll by, birthdays come and go, and finally we find ourselves rich from all the sacrifices we made for Him.

I did not forget about the worries you had this summer and which are still with you. But let us take each day as it comes and leave to Him the many things over which we have no control. For Gabriel, in particular, we must trust that God's plan in having him wait so long is better than ours. I was very happy that M. Traway did not frighten you, he must be a very wise man.

Say a little prayer that Our Lord will bless my new year ahead; I will have some great responsibilities and must bear them all myself; God must make the best possible use of me.[1] I can't wait to get back to Paris to see my little friends in Bourget; I think I will go to see them on the feast of the Rosary.

And then, I'm also planning to see the Cirices, especially Marguerite; I'm happy that Guiguite met her and liked her so well. As for my work, it will be essentially the same and probably will include some parish work during Lent; but I don't know anything yet.

Goodbye for now, Mother; tell Guiguite how much I enjoy her letters and thank her for me. My love to you both.

Pierre

1. See A. Guillermore, *Les Jésuites* (P.U.F., 1961), pp. 114-120, on Fathers Albert Valensin (Auguste's brother) and Teilhard de Chardin.

35

Paris, October 14, 1913

Dear Father and Mother,

Yesterday morning I saw our precious Victor at about seven
o'clock. Even though he still doesn't find Ste. Geneviève very
exciting he looked much better than he did two weeks ago when
I saw him with Father. I tend to think that he'll manage anyway.
The food where he stays is not bad at all and he seems to be eat-
ing plenty of it. Even his cheeks show that he hasn't been under-
nourished! —Yesterday the weather was really beautiful; after
touring the Louvre we saw some sky balloons taking off from
the Gordon-Bennett and float along over the Tuileries, scaring
the pigeons and sending them every which way. We decided to
go back to Vieux-Colombier after the first four were off. From
our window we saw the rest of them being launched. And were
they ever so slow in going about it! Since Father saw me things
are pretty much the same and going fine. Monday I started work
at the Museum again, spending most of my time examining
insect fossils. Boule's come back, too, along with some other
friends of mine. Recently I've been celebrating 6:30 Mass in a

112

catacomb on the Boulevard Raspail. I guess all my work is cut out for me this year.

I've paid a visit to Bourget for the past two Sundays. Maybe it's the new employees or maybe it's the perfectionist they've chosen as administrator, but the orphanage is running smoothly as ever and the kids are the nicest you could hope to find; even little Vaure is there! I couldn't have found a place more at home than with M. Pâris. He's been hunting in the Plaine St. Denise (about eight miles outside of Paris) and he's caught enough partridge and rabbit that you can count them by tens (and that was without "artificial" repopulation)! Is he proud of himself! I was hoping to get this letter to you yesterday, but I didn't have time to finish it until then. That goes to show you how much I am at Vieux-Colombier. Last night M. Boule and I were talking about a few things when we saw a dirigible pass directly over the Museum. It's the closest I've ever seen one of them.

I'll say goodbye for now—my love to both of you. Tell everybody at home I said hello. By the way, Mother, Father Hérodeau reminded me to thank you for the notice about Françoise; he only reproaches her for her restraint in making publicity. What's more, he sent samples of the work to Maduré.

Pierre

36

Paris, October 30, 1913

Dear Father and Mother,

I guess I'm a little behind in writing, but I hope that my letter to Gabriel helped you not to lose patience all together. Besides, there isn't anything to worry about. I've gotten back to the regular "run of the mill" routine and everything is going as it was last year. Right now I'm racking my brains trying to put the finishing touches on my thesis and trying to get it in order once and for all.[1] When I told you that I couldn't wait to get rid of this thesis I didn't mean I was dissatisfied with my work, I was just a little bit too anxious to get it typed up and done with. Last Thursday I finally made up my mind that I was going to see the Museum of Archeology in St. Germain-en-Laye. I took Bovier-Lapierre[2] with me; he's been a professor at Beirut for

1. *Les Carnassiers des phosphorites au Quercy,* a thesis which appeared in the *Annales de Paléontologie,* vol. 9, fasc. 3 and 4, pp. 103–192, with 13 figures, nine engravings, and eight tables (1914–1915). This thesis is to be completed in the following volume (vol. 10, p. 1–20, 1916–1921) as *Sur quelques primates des phosphorites du Quercy* with six figures and two engravings.
2. See *Letters from Egypt,* letter 4.

about a year and he's been a good friend of mine. The chateau up there is beautiful, especially the inner hall. The weather was very cloudy and the sky was very dark which made it hard to get a good view of the grounds. At the museum I saw Abbé Breuil. He has the run of the whole Museum. I got to see everything that could possibly interest me. The Abbé is busy rearranging his collection of weapons and *objets d'art* from pre-historic times, some of which are truly marvelous. Although art is not a main interest of mine, I still found it interesting to be able to see what I've been reading about and what's more to be able to hold them in my own hands. Since I last wrote to you I saw Guillaume de Jerphanion and Father Jalabert,[3] whom I'm sure you probably remember. I was so glad to see a couple of old friends again.

Goodbye for now. Say hello to everybody at home. I'll be thinking especially of the family during the next few days, for I will celebrate Mass for the deceased of the family on All Souls' Day. They are truly our saints. I'm going to see if I can say Mass on the 4th for the family.

Pierre

3. Father Louis Jalabert (1877–1943), Orientalist and editor of the *Etudes,* representative of the University of St. Joseph in Beirut and foreign minister of Paris.

37

Muséum national d'Histoire naturelle
Laboratoire de Paléontologie
3, place Valhubert

Dear Father and Mother,

I'm writing from the Museum so that I won't put off this letter any longer: it's been nearly three weeks now since I have written. Fortunately, Victor is there to give you the news, since we see each other nearly every other Sunday. Since the semester recess began yesterday, I didn't see him at all, as I went on an excursion to Amiens, inspecting the prehistoric findings there. It was under the direction of M. Commont, who's been working at the alluvions of the Somme for a number of years. We visited a series of caves in which flint tools have been discovered. Even though the weather was quite bad, with showers and cold wind, the day was very enjoyable. I think I should tell you who went along with me. There was Dr. Ober-

maier (a good friend since I met him in Santander), a Baron
Blanc (inspector of museums in Rome), and the Count
Bégouën, from Toulouse (he's a pre-historian who discovered,
with his sons, bison depicted on clay in a cave at Ariège.[1] We
had arrived at Amiens Wednesday night and left at 4:30 the
next day. We spent most of our time in the quarries of St.
Acheul and Montières. I was able to get a better look at the town
and the cathedral there, than ever before. A funny thing happened
to me there. I was able to recognize the gallery of Commerce
right off—I remembered it from the time I visited it when I was
ten years old! My visit to the Convent of the Little Sisters of the
Poor[2] was the best. The stuffed nut-hatch arrived without
any damage whatsoever. The Fouasses received it with great
care, and handled it as if it were something sacred. It's been some
years now that not a one has been killed, but this year four have
been stuffed, all coming from the Haute-saone. I remember seeing one at Florennes one year, where it had been killed, stuffed,
and given the title "Siberian thrush."

Last Sunday I went to see M. Pâris since it was his name day
(St. Charles). The little glassmakers put on a short play and
sang songs in his honor. They were as usual very open-hearted
and did everything quite well. I met a second little boy from

1. Count Henri Bégouën (1863–1956), pre-historian, explored with
his three sons the caves of Tuc d'Audoubert and those of Trois Frères
both located in Ariège. They discovered pre-history paintings; the first
depicted two bison, done in clay. One of his sons, Max Henri, knew of
Father Teilhard during the war and they became great friends; he is
mentioned several times in his "mémoire." Count Bégouën would later
lend his name to Father Teilhard, for a story in a work of Edouard Le
Roy: "L'exigence et le fait de l'évolution," in *La Vie Catholique*, September 29, 1928.

2. His sister Françoise had resided there after her novitiate.

Clermont who comes from somewhere around St. Alyre—I can't remember his name off hand.

This morning I received your letter and Guiguite's (I was so glad to hear about Gabriel). From what I hear from Yéyé, let's hope that the United States won't start war with Mexico.[3]

My love to both of you. The same for Guiguite and the boys. I hope Gonzague is keeping at his studies in law.

Pierre

3. Mexico at the time was in the stage of a national crisis of civil war which began in November, 1910, and lasted for nearly ten years. In 1914 it provoked intervention by the United States.

38

Dear Father and Mother,

I'm writing to you on the first day of the semester, it's a little cold, and looks like it's going to snow sooner or later; I wouldn't be surprised if the country near here is already covered with snow. Since I've written to you last, the days have gone by very quickly but without anything unusual or so different that Victor can't tell you about. I was glad that he has made friends with a few young men from Hornoy. Now he has to get himself a tennis racket, if he wants to keep up the good relationship with them and if he wants to get along with his cousins at Point-du-Tour; then, too, I think playing tennis is the best way he can spend his afternoons, they can rent a court there for a very low rate. As for me and my work, nothing new or exciting; I've been sitting quietly with my book, but it's the illustrations for the thesis that are taking so long—not giving me time to do anything else on the side. The printing looks like it'll take a year, the first copy of the *Annales de Paléontologie* (which I have to have published) is so thick![1] Last Monday I received a little bill from the Academy of Science:[2] (I think I'll send it to Gabriel and Joseph and let them have the pleasure (?) of paying it.) I haven't received any assignment to preach for Lent—and I'm kind of happy about it. If I don't get assigned anywhere, I'll have to go down south during June, at least to see the famous Montauban.

Adieu, Father and Mother. All my love to you and Guiguite, Gabriel, Joseph, Gonzague. I'll be praying for you.

Pierre

1. See letter 36.
2. For *Sur une formation de carbono-phosphate de chaux d'âge paléolithique,* from the Academy of Science, December 1, 1913, vol. 157, pp. 1077–1079.

39

Dear Father and Mother,

I was very much annoyed to learn that Father is having trouble with his rheumatism again, and I wish you'd tell me just what's the matter with him, especially what's wrong with his good hand. I had a suspicion something like this was up, when I didn't receive any letter from you on Wednesday or Thursday. I knew then that something was wrong, because you've always written more regularly than I have. Since Gabriel left, Lent has been going along without anything big enough to write you about. I avoided staying up half the night with M. de Margerie by going to see him about six o'clock last night. I was able to speak with him for a while on a very interesting subject, and was able to get to sleep at a decent hour.

As for the society in Paris, I saw Marguerite last Saturday. She's finally lost that little English girl she was teaching. She took it rather hard but managed not to become too depressed. She had to go to Belgium this week, partly to take a rest and partly to see the new "Sion" at Anvers (she can get some ideas for the home at the Institute).[1] They should start building on the 5th of March (break ground, I mean). Gabriel picked out the spot! I think you know that I'm leaving Paris next Friday—with, besides everything else, a very great enthusiasm. You can write to me at M. Chauvin's,[2] 16 Quai Tilsitt. You should hear from me by Saturday. During Easter week I've decided to go to Clermont-Montauban; I'll be in Clermont Tuesday or Wednesday of that week. A friend of mine, Dr. Obermaier, left for Puente-Viesgo (in Santander) with his assistant from Alsace. I was glad to see them again. They're going to go through what they had to last year[3] (this time for five months). It will be the last time they can excavate down there. Glangeaud came down again from the Geological Society;[4] he even told us some interesting things about the Livradois and the Forey. I really became absorbed in it for those few moments.

Goodbye for now. All my love to you, Guiguite and the boys. This morning I didn't forget Albéric's birthday in my Mass.

Pierre

1. The new extension of her Institute. See letter 7.
2. Louis Chauvin, then provincial officer of Lyons.
3. See letters 22 and 25.
4. In 1914 Father Teilhard published an article in the *Bulletin de la Société géologique de France,* titled "Présentation d'échantillons de Quercyte (phospho-carbonate de chaux)," vol. 14, pp. 9–10.

40

Dear Father and Mother,

Here we are again, and another Lent is almost over.[1] Last week I preached ten times to the whole congregation and to the ladies in particular; after this week it will be more or less finished. I'll be preaching to the men three more times (their retreat started yesterday). I'll be all finished during Holy Week. All in all I think my sermons have been pretty good—but that still doesn't give me the inclination to become a preacher. I don't know what makes a good speaker but I do know you have to keep on improving.

The newspapers have been keeping you informed about the Eucharistic Congress going on here. Even though it was called on such short notice, I don't think it will hinder its success in any way. Of all the different ceremonies I only got to see the closing procession, which was very impressive, except for the time it took to move around. There wasn't much room because

---

1. Father Teilhard had been assigned to preach Lenten sermons in a parish in Lyons.

so many people were crowded into the basilica. Lost in the crowd like everyone around me, I was forced to keep moving with it. It was a funny thing to see the bridges over the Saône about two in the morning crowded with people all going in the same direction. After the people received a blessing, a plane flew over the basilica, probably some sort of salute, and was just at the right time so as not to distract the people. The bishop must have sensed it for at that moment he was about to say something but found himself talking to the people's backs . . . they had turned around to look at the sky. The benediction they gave the city was very moving, but only a few could see it due to the Fourvière and the location of the streets along the Rhône and the Saône. A number of people went on their knees when they heard the cannon shots. Everyone seems to regret that they were at first sceptical about having the Congress in Lyons.

It is agreed, in observing their success, that, moreover for reasons unknown, one should have hesitated to reconvene the international Eucharistic Congress of 1914 at Lyons. Lacking the procession of the Blessed Sacrament, one could have marched as in London, and so the Catholics would have counted themselves above the others—while at Lourdes they are alone to see themselves.

Since Sunday it's been very hot. Even Bellecour's chestnut trees have withered and yesterday, taking a trip up to where the Rhône and Saône meet, I admired the color of the fields and weeping willows nearby. Not wanting to let my "paleontological" studies go completely, I went back to see the science faculty again and I'm going to try to get into the Museum of St. Pierre (break down the door, if I have to!). I've been thinking of going to Grive-St-Alban (in Isère); there are a few things I'm interested in seeing there. But who knows? It depends on how I feel. I've only met a few people I know in Mongré; they pointed out a Flachaire from Roustan to me (his name is Bruno and he's about Gabriel's age). M. de Boissieu's wife met me in the sacristy after Mass and told me that M. de Boissieu would try to contact me so we could talk about Father. M. de Judie, another of Father's friends, called, but I wasn't home. He told the curate there who he was and that he was from the Institut Catholique.

Adieu. All my love. Tell Guiguite and the boys I was asking for them. I will probably write before Holy Week ends. I hope to be in Clermont the Monday after Easter. Until then, take care.

Pierre

41

Lyons, April 3, 1914

Dear Father,

Thank you for your letter which came yesterday.

There's nothing new here in Lyons except that I only have to speak seven more times and that we had a deluge yesterday that prevented me from going to Grive-St-Alban. Today it's beautiful out. Wednesday I made a pilgrimage to la Tête-d'Or,[1] which brought back many a forgotten memory.

Adieu, Father—all my love.

My best to all.

Pierre

1. The park of la Tête-d'Or, in Lyons.

42

Dear Father and Mother,

Well, I've been back in Paris since Wednesday night. My trip back hasn't been dull, since I left you Sunday morning. I got to see everything I wanted to at Toulouse and, after spending two days at Montauban, I was convinced that the old relics of the Museum were no longer of any use for me. There was nothing new there that would help me in my work. But I'm not in the least worried about it . . . maybe because I'm lazy. The weather has been great all week except for the little bit of sleet that fell Monday, when I was at Montauban; the countryside up there in Gascony is really something to see. I've never seen Toulouse look so good . . . with all its monuments—outside and inside, the Capitol, and the "Hall of Fame" (which was getting ready to award its prizes for the games just held). I liked the frescos there very much (most of them done by Jean-Paul Laurens), even though a good number of them were painted in a way which lets one see the brush-marks even at a great distance. I was able to see the inside of St. Cernin's Church but

127

I couldn't get down to see the crypt since evening services were being held. I can't write about what I did at Montauban since it wasn't very much except that I felt very much at home there.

I've returned to work at the Museum, as you've probably guessed. M. Boule is at Santander and for a couple of days I won't have to be running in and out of the lab for him and it will be much more quiet now that he is not around! We've been having as good a time as we had last week; I hope the dry air at Sarcenat helps to relieve the pain in Father's legs.

Goodbye for now. All my love to you, Guiguite, and the boys. I'll be praying for you all.

Pierre

43

Dear Father and Mother,

As I'm writing this letter the wind is howling outside and it's terribly cold. You must be having the same thing at Auvergne. Too bad that April weather went so fast. Victor was just here, but he didn't stay long; he went out to play cards with a friend from Marneffe. He looked great, but was a bit tired from staying up so late studying for his philosophy exam. He said that's all he's been doing for the past few days. This afternoon we joined the crowd strolling up and down the Cour-la-Reine after we stopped at Georges' house. The whole street was decked out in its spring finery and it looked very nice. We finished up by seeing the Musée des Arts Décoratifs (the one I saw with Gabriel last winter). The ground floor had an exhibit from England. They had some very beautiful things. There were some beautiful water colors (Guiguite would have enjoyed them), some embroideries and jewels, loaned for the display by the Queen of England. There were even some stuffed rabbits and a few stuffed owls; I was picturing how nice they'd look over the fireplace back home.

In this depressing weather, I don't feel I have the courage to do anything more than going to see the election results made public by the *Démocratie*. Two weeks ago, I was in front of the *Echo de Paris,* at the Place de l'Opera, watching the amusing spectacle of the crowd booing and cheering each new announcement. The photo of Thalamas which was presented from time to time, drew the liveliest response. I had to leave before the unfortunate news came of the victory of Caillaux.[1]

Last Thursday I went to Marguerite's to help out with first communion; Jeanne's maternal instincts were bubbling over that day and her little charges were dressed delightfully; I don't have to tell you that here the ceremony was "performed" in an exemplary fashion—for the last time in this chapel. Next Wednesday I'm going to show Cecile's class around the Museum.

Aside from that nothing is new; I'm drawing and photographing all day long for my next project. Boule seems to have forgotten about the excavations from Rheims and I'm certainly not going to mention them. Maybe if I have time you'll see them a little later. This morning I was at Bourget, as usual. Little Gimbert (who comes from the region of St. Eutrope) is now one of my best friends down there.

Adieu. My love to you, Guiguite, and the boys.

I hope you won't worry about Olivier; when you want, I can get to see him.

Pierre

1. Concerning these elections (April 10, May 10, 1914), see Jacques Chastenet, *Histoire de la Troisième République,* t. 4: *Jours inquiets et Jours sanglants—1957,* pp. 168–170.

44

Paris, May 25, 1914

Dear Father,

Here is a letter which, to use your words, will make you cry
out to heaven, but one which I *must* write: you do what you
want. Here it is: next week you will have the chance to take
Guiguite to see, not a specialist exactly, but a man who, in Paris,
constantly treats the diseases of the nerves and marrow and in
whom—despite his youth—I am assured from three sources, I
could have complete confidence. This doctor is a certain Dr.
Bedel (former intern of Dr. Brissot—this for Planchard—and
one of his top students) presently in the south and who could
come to Paris through Clermont.

For Guiguite it's not a question of having another treatment
but rather to get a diagnosis *to find out what she has*; in the
opinion of all those I've spoken to (without naming anyone,
naturally), it doesn't seem to be tuberculosis of the bone. A relatively quick cure is therefore possible.

It doesn't seem that what I've told you should get you and

131

mother upset: it's no different now than it was to bring Guiguite to Piolet.

Let me know one way or another and it will all be taken care of. Dr. Bedel could be in Clermont Friday evening, the 5th, or the next day. I don't know how much he charges: but since he is young, and just beginning to establish himself, I hope his price will be reasonable. If you want to write to him directly, his address is:

Dr. Maurice Bedel, Terrasse Tressemanes,

Grasse (Alp. Mar.).

Madeleine Georges was very helpful to me but it is I who must take all the responsibility.

It bothered me to write this, since it is a touchy subject with you but it seemed like there was nothing else I could do.

Adieu, all my love to you and mother and I'll write you again tomorrow or the next day as usual.

It's going to be very good to see each other the 10th and 11th of June.

My love to all.

Pierre

45

Dear Father and Mother,

It is very strange to think that within two weeks I will be with you in Sarcenat. Marriages are doing well these days . . . except at each ceremony I must give a little talk and I haven't even written the first line yet! I intend to arrive at Clermont on Tuesday, the 9th, and leave on Friday morning: that will give me at least one day with you.

Since my last letter we've had the choice of it being too hot or too cold . . . as you must know. Nothing has changed here and my work continues to be centered around the Museum. However, the last two Sundays had an added bit of excitement. I went on a geological expedition with my friend Boussac, a professor at the Institut Catholique.

Both times we went to Oise. First, to Chaumont and Chambors, then to Auvers and Beauvais. The day we went to Chaumont was especially beautiful; the hilly countryside stretches for miles and its tall trees are everywhere looking over vast cultivated plains: at this time of year they are completely green.

That alone made our little excursion a delight, not to mention the sea shells we were picking up by the handful which were as "fresh" as if they had been gathered by the seashore. When we arrived in Chambors we were surprised to see that even the tiniest streets had an enamelled plaque with the name of the street on it. Our admiration, however, stopped when we saw election posters which told us that the citizens of this place were under the "enlightened" protection of Bouffandeau.[1]

The weather wasn't as good when we were in Beauvais, but the fossils were just as numerous; we could even see the cathedral from our sand pit. To tell you the truth, I wonder if that isn't the best way to see it . . . emerging, like a colossus, from the midst of a string of closely placed, small and antiquated houses, —as in Bayeux.

Adieu, Father and Mother. And I'll see you soon. I was happy to receive the news about Olivier that Father sent me. My love and prayers to all. My best to Guiguite.

Pierre

1. Felix Bouffandeau (1855–1926), secretary general of the radical and the radical socialist party from 1902–1906; then from 1906 he was Deputy of Oise.

46

Paris, June 28, 1914

Dear Father and Mother,

I haven't written to you since Ranquet's marriage and it's been a long time. Quite a few things have happened since then and some of them are not too pleasant. I didn't know that Guiguite's cast would have been so painful: I hope that Planchard understood Bedel's idea: not that there should be complete immobility, but that the cast should strengthen the spine and still give her as much freedom as possible. Tell me what Planchard says because I'm going to speak to Bedel two weeks from today. I say "two weeks from today" for I know what I'll be doing from now until October. Here is my schedule: on the evening of July 15 I leave for the Alps, and will stay there until August 15. From there I'll return to Paris for about a month. And after that, around September 20 I will be in Hastings and then in Canterbury. I'm looking forward to my trip into the Alps, not only because of the scenery but also because I'll have some good company. We start out in the back hills from a town called Colmars, situated between Digne and Barcelonette; from there we go through Gap and Briançon till we reach Modane, and then we return by way of Maurienne. It will take about ten days. After a few days in Grenoble, which will be my point of attack, we will set out alone, M. Boussac and I, to make a map of the Val d'Isère. I'll give you more details later.

I can't tell you anything more about the cave-ins of the streets here in Paris: Aunt Félicité even telegraphed to see if Uncle Georges had been swallowed up in one of the cracks! Personally I haven't even seen the holes.

Adieu. My love to all.

Pierre

47

Paris, July 12, 1914

Dear Father and Mother,

I thought I'd wait till the last moment before I let you know I was going on a trip. I leave tonight for Grenoble loaded down with mountain climbing equipment—especially spiked shoes that will dig in for a better grip. You probably know already that I plan on spending all day tomorrow with Gabriel. Tuesday we meet at Barcelonette and travel all day by train to Grenoble!

I'll be sending you a few post cards; in any event, don't write me before the 25th. I'll then be back in Grenoble for a three or four-day rest. (the address in Grenoble will be 12 rue Voltaire, at Father Journoud's).[1]

As always happens, this last week has been a merry-go-round of goodbyes and putting things in order.

My love to you, Guiguite, and the boys.

Pierre

1. Father Joseph Journoud, then superior of the Jesuit House of Residence.

48

Allos, Friday

We were here at the lake yesterday and we're going to stay at Gap tonight. Everything is fine. The countryside is magnificent, the geology fascinating, and the companions are charming.

My love to all.

Pierre

49

Montdauphin-Guillestre, Sunday

Everything is still going along quite well. Tomorrow we start up that very high mountain.

The day after tomorrow, we will be in Briançon.

My love to all.

Pierre

50

Briançon (1251 métres d'altitude)
Grand Hôtel-Henri Bonnabel
     Téléph. n°. 11

Dear Father and Mother,

It seems that we are a day ahead of schedule and because of the bad weather I can give you a few more details than usual. First of all, everything is going along perfectly: yesterday we walked from four in the morning till eight at night, climbing nearly 10,000 feet and we didn't feel tired at all. I'm even improving my shape with all this exercise.

For the past week I've been living in the midst of a magnificently beautiful country. You get used to it very quickly; it seems to me that if you really want to enjoy the Alps you should go through them as a naturalist or else find some beautiful spot to settle down in so that you can slowly drink in its charm and better understand it all.

In the lower Alps the most beautiful spot I've ever seen is

without a doubt the lake of Allos. I sent you a postcard of it.
The water was a sparkling green hue, guarded over by the rocks
which you saw, and bordered by superb meadows in which I've
begun to enjoy the luxury of the alpine flora (among which I
was happy to see the arnica again!). I really do enjoy this section of the Alps. The light and the cicadas remind you of
Provence and you can stay in real family-style inns. We finally
left in a car which was rented for us and took the "Alpine
road," served by the P.L.M. At the bend separating the basin
of Verdon from Ubaye we got out and walked a bit and actually
saw a grouse. The woods dissolve into wide open spaces so
quickly that it seems that the game disappears with it . . . no
matter how hard you try to see any.

We went through Barcelonette with its "Mexican" villas like
lightning and suddenly found ourselves at Gap which is very
different. I was wearing my heavy coat, a knapsack, and my
enormous shoes, borrowed from the preacher the year before.
The curate received me very warmly and his mother once again
was most kind; I really enjoyed going back there. But it was
only for one night. The next morning we were in Guillestre,
near Montdauphin, in the Quayras, a little above Embrun. It
was from there I sent you a card as we started out on a hot but
very interesting expedition, during which I saw a number of
Parnassius (some with red spots, others without). But I couldn't
get any of them. From Guillestre we went to Vallouise, a group
of chalets located in the valley of the same name at the foot of
the Pelvoux; it was there that Lesdiguières massacred the
Vaudois.[1]

1. The Vaudois had moved into the French side of the Alps in the
thirteenth century, in the val Freissinière, the val Argentière, and the

Yesterday's trip took us from there to Briançon to climb up the huge Sablier, which isn't too well-known but held some geological interests for us. From then on, time seemed to fly by. From the summit we had a very beautiful, but far from complete, view of Pelvoux; it even started to snow and as it landed on the ferns it made a very delightful picture; the guide showed us some woodchuck and mountain goat tracks in the snow. We came down through a typical alpine valley, bordered by larch-trees with a rug of rhododendrons, and at the bottom was a thick green pasture in which almost a hundred cows would ring their little bells as they moved about.

As you already know, Briançon is a very picturesque town, encircled by the fortifications of Vauban, and it has a number of alpine clubs; but it's raining so much today I wouldn't try going out at all. After looking at my "celebret" this morning—that precious piece of paper that I kept on my person—the vicar immediately asked me if I was a relative of Lieutenant Teilhard.

Tomorrow, we're driving to Oulx (Italy) by way of Geneva and will stay over night in Modane. All that remains, then, will be Maurienne. We'll be in Grenoble Friday night; you already know that I must stay there three or four days. Will I see Gabriel?

I eagerly await news from you.

My love to all and I will remember you in my prayers.

Pierre

---

val Louise. In the sixteenth century, through the influence of Guillaume Farel, some of them converted to Calvinism.

The Duke de Lesdiguières (1543–1626), captain of Henry IV, one of the leaders of the reform party, became governor of Dauphine, and in 1622 was converted to Catholicism.

51

Dear Father and Mother,

I've been back in Grenoble since Thursday night—I know I should have written sooner than this. I probably won't be leaving before August 1. In my last letter, from Briançon, I told you that the rains had started; from then on things started to be spoiled for our expedition. It rained the whole way from Briançon to Oulx. The clouds covered up the tops of the mountains but let us see just enough of the rocks we were looking for. What we saw, essentially, of Italy, was a dreadfully gray sky —an uninterrupted stream of batteries and soldiers, more or less orderly, making for the Alpine forts—and some macaroni in the inn where we stopped. When we took the train through Mont-Cenis that evening, the torrential rains began to cause serious mud slides and we were only in Modane an hour when the "Charmaix" cut off the road on the French side and completely flooded the lower town. I would never have believed water could be so powerful if I hadn't seen it for myself. The next morning it was both tragic and rather amusing to see the station filled with broken-down trains and stranded travelers; the students at Bolengo College, which had closed for vacation that day, returned to Turin to go by way of Vintimille. There were so many emigrants, loaded down with luggage, who were trying to get to the next station in the hope of getting a train. Therefore, shortening our stay and leaving half our bags at the hotel, we decided to do the same thing. Thus I arrived in Grenoble a day ahead of schedule, after moving through St. Jean de Maurienne. Up until the last moment we wondered if we would make it. Along the opulent valley of Graisivaudan the train was at times cut off by water which had seeped into the wheat fields and was so deep that it was as high as the wheat itself. It seemed that the flooding of the Drac up above was even worse.

I saw Gabriel on Friday night. He gave me all your letters and news; Saturday morning I accompanied him to the train for St. Geoire; he seemed perfectly happy. I still don't know if my second trip will be delayed. I spend my time seeing the museums, correcting some proofs, and also trying to write a little talk about marriage. But that doesn't take all day and I sure will be happy to get my knapsack and climbing shoes back on.

Adieu. My love and prayers to you and everyone at home.

Pierre

52

Grenoble, Saturday [August 1, 1914][1]

Dear Father and Mother,

I leave for Paris tonight, where I left my military pass and where I'm supposed to live. From there it is very likely that I'll wind up in Riom.

My best to you both and be brave.

Pierre

1. General mobilization had just been announced by the Council of Ministers, assembled in the Elysée Palace.

53

Dear Father and Mother,

I hope you have received my card from Grenoble where I told you I was returning to Paris to pick up my pass and await my call to service. I took the last train leaving for Paris before the mobilization, so there were many delays but also many picturesque sights. The track was completely guarded by local patriots who were heroically funny with their fatigues and their pots. It was most difficult to get from the railroad station in Lyons to the rue du Vieux-Colombier; the cabs and taxis were gone, the buses had been requisitioned, the trolleys were down by three-quarters and the subway was completely off schedule. The city too was completely changed; but it was reassuring to see people leaving with their little knapsacks, unaffected and quite happy. They told me at the police station that I would have to wait here in Paris for my own orders to move out, —which will come, I imagine, in five or six days. I hope to be put in a position where I may be of some use.

Yesterday, to keep myself busy, I went to Uncle Georges, but arrived just a little too late and missed him. I then went to see Uncle Cirice. I was surprised to find Marguerite there, who had, with good reason, cut short her vacation, not wanting to leave Paris where she wished to convert the Institution Notre Dame des Champs into a shelter. I'm sending you this letter through a friend, Father Boudou,[1] who is leaving for Clermont tonight.

I naturally would like to know what's happening to Gabriel, Joseph, and Gonzague.

Adieu. You know what I pray for you all. Don't let Mother worry too much, at least not about me.

I thought about Loulou's birthday today.

Pierre

Yesterday, on the rue du Regard, I met a brilliant teacher: they told me (too late) that he was Father Vigy, just stationed in Cherbourg.

Ordinations were held yesterday morning at Ore Place and Enghien (exceptionally early this year); several young priests had to leave before saying their first Mass.

1. Father Adrien Boudou (1876–1945), from Auvergne, was a professor of holy Scripture at Enghien and Tananarive. He was published by Beauchesne's in the "Collection Verbum Salutis," directed by Father Huby: *Les Actes des Apôtres* (1933); *Les Jésuites à Madagascar au XIXe siècle,* 2 vol. (1940), and before (1935) the first biography of the martyr: *Le Père Jacques Berthieu (1838–1896),* who was beatified in 1965.

54

Paris, August 9, 1914

Dear Father and Mother,

The correspondence between here and Clermont is most assuredly regular, judging by the promptness with which your letters have arrived; only Joseph's card is missing which must be trying to catch up with me in Grenoble.

You will notice, first of all, that I'm back here again, though I'm afraid it won't be for a very long time. They aren't talking about mobilizing the inactive reserves yet, of which I am a member, except to send them out to harvest (!), if things get much worse.[1] It's impossible to enter the least kind of ambulance or other service; you have to stay put and wait to be called, which may never happen! There are some good reasons justifying it all but it is frustrating to have to remain where you are and do nothing, when only two weeks ago you showed you were able to be on a mountain every day for 13 hours a day and didn't get tired at all.

I had to give up such hopes of active duty and am back at the

1. Pierre Teilhard had not yet served actively in the army.

148

Museum, which is quite deserted now; M. Boule is doing the same thing.

The only thing missing around here are the trolleys; but on the other hand, when you are walking along the streets, you are happily surprised to find you can get across and even walk in the streets that were "deadly" before.

It seems that the wounded are beginning to come into Paris; but up to now the military hospitals and nursing homes have been able to accommodate them all. Marguerite has very generously accepted the ladies from Sion to come and help staff the shelter of Notre Dame des Champs; but it may be some time before each gets a chance to practice, there have been so many offers to help. Send me Gonzague's address.

Goodbye for now. I love you and pray for you and all those who are gone. Take courage!

You must be very proud to have Gabriel down there.

A thousand good wishes to Guiguite.

Pierre

55

Dear Father and Mother,

There is nothing new here, except a few newly created chaplains. There is nothing to do and I am presently resigned to wait and see what happens to me. I don't even have agriculture to fall back on the way Joseph does. So, egoistically, I fill up my time with fossils. My life here is back to what it was two months ago; even the trolleys are on schedule again!

After the first few days the excitement wore off and now Paris is rather gloomy; all you see are people reading newspapers (editions keep coming out one right after the other all day long), and wringing dry any of the news in the *communiqués,* so parsimoniously distilled by the ministry. The military cars in the city and the bombs exploding in the air all night are the only positive evidence that there is a war going on here. Please heaven that during these beautiful days, when they have the time to think things over, the government will take steps to stop this dreadful plague that is upon us.

The wounded are not coming to Paris and the good will of

the people is beginning to show itself to the needs of the poor and especially towards the children. They are thinking of taking the children to Notre Dame des Champs for the day.

I hope you will eventually get some news about Gabriel; here they are beginning to hear about letters arriving from the East quite often. I would like to know what Olivier is doing. Mother must hope that his work will keep him in Boléo.

Adieu, Father and Mother. I love you both. My best to Guiguite whose long letter I received this morning. Be assured that the soldiers in our family are remembered at all my Masses.

Pierre

56

Paris, September 11, 1914

DEAR Father and Mother,

Ten more days have gone by in this terrible war that is making three-quarters of Europe suffer. With the help of God it may soon be over. I hope our family will not be affected by it too much!

You won't be surprised to learn that everything is the same here; but with Millerand it seems like the reserves will be called up any day now. I can't wait to get my assignment. I'm ready to do anything for the cause. Farmers, on the other hand, like Joseph, should be kept where they are as long as possible. I hope he will be one of the last to go.

Eight days ago when the Germans were in Compiègne, Paris was quite interesting. Not to mention the German planes (*Tauben*[1]) which I saw strafing the city, the confusion of people leaving the suburbs, despite its sadness, added a picturesque note to it all. The exodus of people afraid to stay in Paris made

1. A German word meaning *pigeon* used during World War I to indicate a German monoplane.

the streets and railroad station a weird spectacle of confusion but there was definitely no panic or disorder; just crowds. The Institut Notre Dame des Champs has become a shelter for refugees and kept me busy a couple of afternoons.

Now we're just waiting for the wounded to arrive; aside from that the city is as calm as could be expected. Every delinquent and gangster has been out of Paris right from the start of the war; never have people been kinder to one another. So, don't let Mother worry about all the confusion up here.

If you have to feel sorry for anyone, it should be the poor little children; people started taking them in everywhere since the schools were closed eight days ago. But it's becoming more and more difficult now that the refugees are piling up.

One of my best friends here finally got across Paris. He was appointed as chaplain two weeks ago; he and all the others on the front line are in very great danger, but it must really be exciting. It makes me sick to have to sit around waiting for my "call!"

I think even Mother would agree with that. But as always, we must obey God's will.

Adieu. My love to you both.

Be brave!

Pierre

57

Paris, September 17, 1914

Dear Father,

This is just a note to support Victor in his request to join the army. I realize you may not like this. The poor boy has just written me a very disturbing letter and I think I know how he feels. Now that he is to become a soldier it is very unfair to put obstacles in his way. To hold him back now may interfere with his whole career. Not to have fought in 1914, because of a 24-hour difference in age, could only be a bad beginning for an officer. There are, naturally, some great risks by enlisting now but these are risks which will strengthen the man for life, and on which his career depends, —not to mention the honor it will bring to the family. I'm afraid that if you kept Victor back for too long, he would become depressed and dejected; most assuredly he would always regret it. If, however, he does go (or at least tries to enlist) he will never regret it.

So, once more I must make you and Mother face another difficult sacrifice; but what am I doing except to tell you what

154

you already know and which is as inevitable as are all the other villainous things happening to us today?

Of course, I defer my opinion to that of my other brothers who are more versed in military matters than I; Olivier's opinion would be most helpful; if, however, it has to take a month or two to come, it would be better not to wait.

May God show you the light and help you in making this difficult decision. I love you very much. And I'm sorry if I've caused you any sorrow.

Pierre

58

Paris, September 24, 1914

Dear Mother,

When I returned from driving Olivier to meet his train I found a note telling me to begin my third year[1] "in attendance" at Canterbury.

1. The "Third Year" is another time for recently ordained Jesuits, who have completed their studies and who are not yet active in the apostolic ministry, to go on a long retreat and then take their final vows. Pierre Teilhard then went to England and there under the direction of Father Joseph Daniel, former provincial from Paris, he spent thirty days completing the *Spiritual Exercises* of St. Ignatius. Hardly had this silent retreat ended, when he learned that his brother Gonzague, at the age of 20, had been killed on the field of honor during an attack upon one of the trenches.

"May God's will be done and may His kingdom be our final goal. This is the important thing," he wrote his parents. "You could not dream of a more beautiful ideal for your son than for him to give up his life as a true Christian in one of the greatest tasks this century has yet seen and which shall probably be spoken of throughout history . . ." (December 23, 1914).

Having been declared "fit for military service," he himself was drafted in December and assigned to the 13th division of the medical corps, then stationed in Clermont. It was not long before he was at the front serving as a stretcher-bearer.

I leave tomorrow morning via Dieppe-Folkestone; I don't know if they'll let me stay. . . . It seems most unlikely, then, that I'll see Olivier again before I leave. I was lucky to have seen him now.

My love to all.

Pierre